OPPOSING
VIEWPOINTS®
SERIES

The Music Industry

Other Books of Related Interest:

At Issue Series

Should Music Lyrics Be Censored?

Issues That Concern You

Consumer Culture
Social Networking

"Congress shall make no law … abridging the freedom of speech, or of the press."

First Amendment to the US Constitution

The basic foundation of our democracy is the First Amendment guarantee of freedom of expression. The Opposing Viewpoints Series is dedicated to the concept of this basic freedom and the idea that it is more important to practice it than to enshrine it.

The Music Industry

Noah Berlatsky, Book Editor

GREENHAVEN PRESS
A part of Gale, Cengage Learning

GALE
CENGAGE Learning

Detroit • New York • San Francisco • New Haven, Conn • Waterville, Maine • London

Elizabeth Des Chenes, *Managing Editor*

© 2012 Greenhaven Press, a part of Gale, Cengage Learning

Gale and Greenhaven Press are registered trademarks used herein under license.

For more information, contact:
Greenhaven Press
27500 Drake Rd.
Farmington Hills, MI 48331-3535
Or you can visit our Internet site at gale.cengage.com.

For product information and technology assistance, contact us at:

Gale Customer Support, 1-800-877-4253.
For permission to use material from this text or product, submit all requests online at www.cengage.com/permissions.

Further permissions questions can be emailed to permissionrequest@cengage.com.

Articles in Greenhaven Press anthologies are often edited for length to meet page requirements. In addition, original titles of these works are changed to clearly present the main thesis and to explicitly indicate the author's opinion. Every effort is made to ensure the Greenhaven Press accurately reflects the original intent of the authors. Every effort has been made to trace the owners of copyrighted material.

Cover Image © iStockphoto/Thinkstock/Getty Images.

LIBRARY OF CONGRESS CATALOGING-IN-PUBLICATION DATA

The music industry / Noah Berlatsky, book editor.
    p. cm. -- (Opposing viewpoints)
   Includes bibliographical references and index.
   ISBN 978-0-7377-5743-9 (hardcover) -- ISBN 978-0-7377-5744-6 (pbk.)
  1. Music trade. I. Berlatsky, Noah.
   ML3790.M728 2012
   338.4'778--dc23

                                                     2011032934

Printed in the United States of America
2 3 4 5 6   16 15 14 13 12
FD089

Contents

Chapter 3: What Role Do Record Labels Play in the Twenty-First Century?

Chapter 4: Will Changes in the Industry Hurt Music?

Why Consider Opposing Viewpoints?

> *"The only way in which a human being can make some approach to knowing the whole of a subject is by hearing what can be said about it by persons of every variety of opinion and studying all modes in which it can be looked at by every character of mind. No wise man ever acquired his wisdom in any mode but this."*
>
> *John Stuart Mill*

In our media-intensive culture it is not difficult to find differing opinions. Thousands of newspapers and magazines and dozens of radio and television talk shows resound with differing points of view. The difficulty lies in deciding which opinion to agree with and which "experts" seem the most credible. The more inundated we become with differing opinions and claims, the more essential it is to hone critical reading and thinking skills to evaluate these ideas. Opposing Viewpoints books address this problem directly by presenting stimulating debates that can be used to enhance and teach these skills. The varied opinions contained in each book examine many different aspects of a single issue. While examining these conveniently edited opposing views, readers can develop critical thinking skills such as the ability to compare and contrast authors' credibility, facts, argumentation styles, use of persuasive techniques, and other stylistic tools. In short, the Opposing Viewpoints Series is an ideal way to attain the higher-level thinking and reading skills so essential in a culture of diverse and contradictory opinions.

In addition to providing a tool for critical thinking, Opposing Viewpoints books challenge readers to question their own strongly held opinions and assumptions. Most people form their opinions on the basis of upbringing, peer pressure, and personal, cultural, or professional bias. By reading carefully balanced opposing views, readers must directly confront new ideas as well as the opinions of those with whom they disagree. This is not to argue simplistically that everyone who reads opposing views will—or should—change his or her opinion. Instead, the series enhances readers' understanding of their own views by encouraging confrontation with opposing ideas. Careful examination of others' views can lead to the readers' understanding of the logical inconsistencies in their own opinions, perspective on why they hold an opinion, and the consideration of the possibility that their opinion requires further evaluation.

Evaluating Other Opinions

To ensure that this type of examination occurs, Opposing Viewpoints books present all types of opinions. Prominent spokespeople on different sides of each issue as well as well-known professionals from many disciplines challenge the reader. An additional goal of the series is to provide a forum for other, less known, or even unpopular viewpoints. The opinion of an ordinary person who has had to make the decision to cut off life support from a terminally ill relative, for example, may be just as valuable and provide just as much insight as a medical ethicist's professional opinion. The editors have two additional purposes in including these less known views. One, the editors encourage readers to respect others' opinions—even when not enhanced by professional credibility. It is only by reading or listening to and objectively evaluating others' ideas that one can determine whether they are worthy of consideration. Two, the inclusion of such viewpoints encourages the important critical thinking skill of objectively evaluating an author's credentials and bias. This evaluation will illuminate an author's reasons for taking a particular stance on an issue and will aid in readers' evaluation of the author's ideas.

It is our hope that these books will give readers a deeper understanding of the issues debated and an appreciation of the complexity of even seemingly simple issues when good and honest people disagree. This awareness is particularly important in a democratic society such as ours in which people enter into public debate to determine the common good. Those with whom one disagrees should not be regarded as enemies but rather as people whose views deserve careful examination and may shed light on one's own.

Thomas Jefferson once said that "difference of opinion leads to inquiry, and inquiry to truth." Jefferson, a broadly educated man, argued that "if a nation expects to be ignorant and free . . . it expects what never was and never will be." As individuals and as a nation, it is imperative that we consider the opinions of others and examine them with skill and discernment. The Opposing Viewpoints Series is intended to help readers achieve this goal.

David L. Bender and Bruno Leone,
Founders

Introduction

"[A dispute between Warner Music
and YouTube] has raised anew
questions about the meaning of fair
use under copyright law in the context
of the digital age, when anyone can
easily excerpt copyrighted works and
distribute the result in a manner that is
sometimes hard to identify as being a
commercial product."

> Tim Arango, media business
> journalist

The video-sharing website YouTube was created in 2005. YouTube quickly became extremely popular. Jefferson Graham, writing in a November 21, 2005, *USA Today* article reported that, less than a year after launch, YouTube had more than two hundred thousand registered users and was showing more than 2 million videos per day. According to statistics on the *Website Monitoring Blog*, by July 2006, it was showing 100 million videos per day—numbers that prompted Google to purchase the site for $1.65 billion. In October 2009, YouTube reached 1 billion views per day. Less than a year later, in May 2010, it reached 2 billion views per day.

As YouTube has expanded, it (and other, smaller video-sharing sites like Vimeo and Hulu) have had an enormous effect on the music industry. A survey released in 2011 found that more than 60 percent of people watched music videos on computer, compared with only 20 percent who said they legally downloaded music. This survey "reinforced the role of YouTube as a key platform for music consumption," according to a January 14, 2011, post on *Music Ally* blog.

YouTube's importance reinvigorated the music video as a central promotional tool. In the 1980s and 1990s, videos shown on television stations like MTV had been a central marketing technique for artists. Performers like Michael Jackson had even given the music video some artistic respectability. By 2000, however, videos had declined in popularity. Neil Vidyarthi, writing in a September 23, 2010, article on the Social Times website, explained that, "this led to what can only be called the dark years of music video. Between 2000 and 2005, there really wasn't a single place to tune in and see a whole lot of music videos. MTV was inundated with television shows, and video on the web still wasn't accessible by the mainstream."

YouTube changed all that. As Vidyarthi says, "The user-uploaded video service jumped on the scene and with it came mountains and mountains of content, and included in that was pretty much every music video ever made."

Music videos have, then, become one of the most powerful marketing devices in the current music industry. As an example, in 2007 (just two years after YouTube launched) the band OK Go put up a video for its song "Here It Goes Again." The video showed the band dancing on treadmills. It was an immense hit, catapulting the band to fame; by March 2010 it had been viewed 50 million times. David Kaplan, writing in a February 21, 2010, article on paidContent.org said that the "band's success appeared to point the way for a new way to promote music."

YouTube also pointed the way for new conflicts over revenue. Videos on the site were uploaded by users and were shown for free. In general, no permission was obtained from copyright holders, and no money went to the rights holders when the videos were viewed. YouTube and the labels that owned the rights to the videos struggled to find a way to keep the videos available while generating income for the rights holders. Eventually, they settled on an agreement where YouTube would pay a small amount to copyright owners each time someone streamed a video.

This agreement satisfied some of the record companies. However, it raised other problems. YouTube only paid the record companies for video streams when they were streamed directly from the site. Videos which were embedded—that is, taken from YouTube and placed on other sites—generated no income for the record company. Some record companies, like OK Go's label EMI, demanded that the embedding feature on YouTube be disabled on their videos. But OK Go had relied on users embedding the videos and spreading them far and wide to promote the band. "When EMI disabled embedding, views of 'the treadmill video' . . . dropped 90 percent," according to Kaplan. The dispute over embedding on YouTube was so contentious that it led OK Go to split with EMI, as Daniel Kreps reported in a March 10, 2010, *Rolling Stone* article. Labels, bands, and video sites continue to negotiate the use of music videos on the web.

The rest of this book will examine other ways in which changes in technology and other factors have affected record labels, artists, and others in the music industry. Topics are addressed in the following chapter-title questions: What Copyright Issues Does the Music Industry Face? How Should the Music Industry Respond to the Changing Market? What Role Do Record Labels Play in the Twenty-First Century? and Will Changes in the Industry Hurt Music? Different authors offer varying viewpoints on how music is changing and how the industry should respond.

OPPOSING
VIEWPOINTS®
SERIES

CHAPTER 1

What Copyright Issues Does the Music Industry Face?

Chapter Preface

Mashups are studio-created tracks that combine the vocals from one song with the music from another song. For example, the mashup artist DJ Schmolli combined vocals from pop star Robyn's 2010 hit "Dancing on My Own" with the music from rock band AC/DC's '70s hit "You Shook Me All Night Long" to created a song he called "Dancing On My Own All Night Long." One of the most famous mash-ups is an album-long creation by DJ Danger Mouse called *The Grey Album*, which combined elements of the Beatles' *White Album* with elements from hip hop artist Jay-Z's *The Black Album*.

Mashups are controversial. They are generally composed entirely of other people's songs; that is, the creator of the mashups (like DJ Danger Mouse) do not have the right to the songs they combine. Are mashups illegal?

Ali Golomb argues that mashups are both legal and creative. Writing on December 2, 2008, at *Ward's Kitchen*, a blog for American University's Global Media learning community, Golomb argues that a famous mashup artist named Girl Talk is "taking parts of songs from other artists, but he is engineering them in a specific way that is different from the artist's original intent." Golomb says that this is "still every bit as creative and innovative as the music of past generations," and that it therefore deserves the same respect and legal protection as other forms of art.

Ryan B., in a February 4, 2010, post on the *Yale Law & Technology* blog, agrees in part. He argues that "by pairing up samples from different songs, mashup can provide an entirely new context for the original works. In this way, mashup artists can provide critical commentary on those works, expressing their own perspectives on the songs being utilized." As an example, Ryan B. talks about mashup artist Milkman's "All About It," which combines vocals from rap artist Pitbull's "Go Girl" with the '90s pop song "Another Night" by Real McCoy. Ryan B. says that the new music shows how silly Pitbull's lyrics are. Therefore, the new track comments on, or critiques, Pitbull's song. As a result, Ryan B. says, Milkman's mashup should be protected under the First Amendment, in the same way that parodies are protected. They fall under fair use provisions—that is, mashups use other copyrighted material in a way that is a fair use, not an illegal use.

Kevin McBride at the site *McBride Law, PC*, however, argues in a February 28, 2010, post that mashups in many cases may not be protected by fair use provisions. McBride notes that most mashups do not have an obvious critical component and so would not function as commentary or parody. He concludes that "unquestionably, mashup and digital sampling music compilations require significant creative talent. However what is the *nature* of the talent involved? It seems that the talent is in compilation. The mashup artist has a creative skill to compile underlying works in a new and original way."

McBride concludes that in most cases, unless mashup artists under current law obtain permission from the copyright holders, they are effectively operating illegally.

The following viewpoints examine other copyright issues raised by new technologies.

> "Weaker copyright protection . . . has
> benefited society."

File-Sharing Has Weakened Copyright— and Helped Society

Nate Anderson

Nate Anderson is a senior editor at Ars Technica, *a technology website. In the following viewpoint he reports on the work of Felix Oberholzer-Gee and Koleman Strumpf, two academics who claim that illegal file sharing has not hurt creativity. Oberholzer-Gee and Strumpf argue that the number of books, music, and films created has skyrocketed since file sharing was created. Anderson concludes that, while file sharing hurts music labels, it does not seem to hurt music. Since copyright laws are meant to foster creativity, and since weaker copyright appears to encourage more creativity, Anderson argues that copyright laws in the United States should be relaxed.*

As you read, consider the following questions:

1. According to the US Constitution, as cited by Anderson, what is the purpose of copyright?
2. By how much did the publication of new books rise in the period 2002–2007, as reported by the author?
3. What evidence does IFPI use, according to Anderson, to attempt to demonstrate that file sharing hurts creativity?

Has file-sharing helped society? Looked at from the narrow perspective of existing record labels, the question must seem absurd; profits have dropped sharply in the years since tools like Napster first appeared. But a pair of well-known academics argue peer-to-peer file sharing has weakened copyright in the US . . . and [yet] managed to benefit all of us at the same time.

"Consumer welfare increased substantially due to new technology," write Felix Oberholzer-Gee of Harvard and Koleman Strumpf of the University of Kansas. "Weaker copyright protection, it seems, has benefited society."

Weaker Is Stronger?

Peer-to-peer file-sharing on the Internet has certainly weakened copyright, but that's not necessarily a bad thing unless one equates "stronger copyright" with "better copyright." According to the US Constitution, copyright is about promoting "the Progress of Science and useful Arts"; it's not about enriching authors, except as a means of promoting said "Progress."

When we think about copyright, the most pertinent question to ask is not whether some change would produce less money for rightsholders, but whether some change would *remove incentives to create*. Has file-sharing reduced creators' incentives?

Oberholzer-Gee and Strumpf presented a recent paper at a music business conference in Vienna that tried to answer this question empirically. By charting the production of new books, new music albums, and new feature films over the last decade, the authors tried to see whether creative output went up or down in correlation with file-sharing.

"Data on the supply of new works are consistent with our argument that file sharing did not discourage authors and publishers," they write in their paper "File-sharing and Copyright."

"The publication of new books rose by 66 percent over the 2002–2007 period. Since 2000, the annual release of new music albums has more than doubled, and worldwide feature film

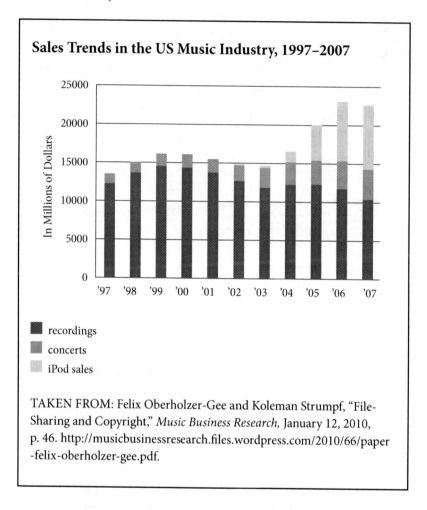

Sales Trends in the US Music Industry, 1997–2007

recordings
concerts
iPod sales

TAKEN FROM: Felix Oberholzer-Gee and Koleman Strumpf, "File-Sharing and Copyright," *Music Business Research*, January 12, 2010, p. 46. http://musicbusinessresearch.files.wordpress.com/2010/66/paper-felix-oberholzer-gee.pdf.

production is up by more than 30 percent since 2003. . . . In our reading of the evidence there is little to suggest that the new technology has discouraged artistic production. Weaker copyright protection, it seems, has benefited society."

The authors don't claim (anymore) that file-sharing has no effect on industries like recorded music. Though both authors also collaborated on a now-famous paper from 2007 which argued that file-sharing had no appreciable impact on music sales, they are willing to concede now that it might be a small part of the industry's problems.

Indeed, they round up a host of studies from the past few years suggesting that, on average, one-fifth of declining music sales might be chalked up to piracy. (The rise of new entertainment options like video games has also hurt the business, and consumers finally stopped "re-buying" old albums on CD by the mid-2000s.)

But looking at such declines provides only a narrow view. Looked at more broadly, the music industry "has grown considerably" in the last few years. When concert revenue is added to recorded music revenue, the authors note that the overall industry grew more than 5 percent between 1997 and 2007.

That's in large part because consumers' willingness to pay for "complements" like concerts and merchandise goes up as the price of music and movies falls, and because consumers are exposed to many more artists when prices are low or nonexistent.

Even if the music industry was shrinking, though, the authors point out that creativity has not declined—which suggests that weaker copyright can still promote the "Progress" sought by the Founders.

"We do not yet have a full understanding of the mechanisms by which file-sharing may have altered the incentives to produce entertainment," conclude the authors. "However, in the industry with the largest purported impact—music—consumer access to recordings has vastly improved since the advent of file-sharing. Since 2000, the number of recordings produced has more than doubled. In our view, this makes it difficult to argue that weaker copyright protection has had a negative impact on artists' incentives to be creative."

Unconvinced

The music industry doesn't buy the argument. According to international trade group IFPI, "Live performance earnings are generally more to the benefit of veteran, established acts, while it is the younger, developing acts, without lucrative live careers, who do not have the chance to develop their reputation through recorded music sales." Thus, recorded music sales remain important.

And IFPI's 2010 "Digital Music Report" makes the case that artists are producing less in states with high piracy rates. "In France, there has been a striking fall in the number of local repertoire albums released in recent years," says the report. "In the first half of 2009, 107 French-repertoire albums were released, 60 per cent down on the 271 in the same period of 2003." (This number appears to involve only major labels, however, and cheap digital tools mean that much of the music production today is done without a major label.)

Even Oberholzer-Gee and Strumpf admit that their findings aren't clear. It could be that, thanks to all these cheap digital tools, even more recordings would have been produced in the US were it not for file-sharing. But when the same trend holds true among book publishers, filmmakers, and musicians—the 2000s were about ever-increasing content—perhaps P2P isn't "disincentivizing" anyone at all.

And if it's not, the entire paper asks by implication, why don't politicians even consider weakening US copyright law?

> *"Illegal file-sharing has . . . had a very significant, and sometimes disastrous, impact on investment in artists and local repertoire."*

Illegal File Sharing Hurts Musicians and Society

IFPI

The International Federation of the Phonographic Industry (IFPI) is the organization that represents the interests of the recording industry worldwide. In the following viewpoint, IFPI argues that file sharing and illegal downloading of music has devastated music sales. The organization says that loss of sales has reduced investment in and development of artists, especially in places like France, Spain, and Brazil, where copyright protection is weak. IFPI warns that although file sharing's first impact was on music, other industries like film, books, and even travel are now being affected as well. This article represents an excerpt from the longer original report.

As you read, consider the following questions:

1. According to IFPI, what reason do most file sharers give for getting their music through file sharing?

IFPI, "Competing in a Rigged Market—The Problem of Illegal File Sharing," *IFPI Digital Music Report 2010*, 2010. www.ifpi.org/content/library/DMR2010.pdf, pp.18–21. Article is an excerpt and does not constitute the whole original report. Reproduced by permission.

2. How does the author say that file sharing has affected the music industry in Brazil?

3. What does Simon Renshaw, as quoted by IFPI, say he fears will happen in the future because of file sharing?

Music companies and legitimate music services are trying to build their online business in a rigged market deluged by unauthorised free content. The growth of illegal file-sharing has been a major factor in the decline in legitimate music sales over the last decade, with global industry revenues down around 30 per cent from 2004 to 2009. In virtually every country of the world, spending on recorded music has fallen since illegal file-sharing became widespread.

Piracy Hurts Sales

All but a few of the independent surveys confirm that the net impact of illegal file-sharing is to reduce spending on legitimate music. Most academic studies exploring the dramatic fall in sales of recorded music conclude that the damage caused by illegal file-sharing is a major factor in the decline. . . .

A 2006 study by Professor Stan Liebowitz, *File-Sharing: Creative Destruction or Just Plain Destruction?* concludes: "The papers that have examined the impact of file-sharing can be categorised by result and by methodology. By result the classification is quite simple. There is one study (Oberholzer and Strumpf, 2004) that claims to find a zero impact but it has been frequently discredited. All the other studies find some degree of negative relationship between file-sharing and sales of sound recordings." Research from Harris Interactive in 2009 among 3,400 online consumers aged 16–54 in the UK highlighted that nearly one in four P2P [peer-to-peer] file-sharers (24%) typically spend nothing on music, while also finding an overlap of legal and illegal downloading among some file-sharers.

A Jupiter Research study in five European countries among 5,000 internet users aged 15 and over in 2009 found that, although there is an overlap between the habits of online music buyers and file-sharers, most illegal file-sharers "do not buy music and are nearly half as likely as music buyers to buy CDs in a High Street [a Britishism for "retail district"] shop or from an online store." The study also finds that the net effect of illegal file-sharing is negative. "Although it is possible that file-sharing functions as some sort of discovery tool for those digital music buyers that also file-share, it is reasonable to assume that their spend would be higher if they were not file-sharing. The overall impact of file sharing on music spending is negative."

A separate body of research helps explain why illegal file-sharing is having this impact on consumer behaviour, confirming the main driver of piracy to be not better choice or quality, but the "lure of free". Researchers GFK found that "because it's free" was the main answer given among over 400 illegal file-sharers in research unveiled in Sweden in July 2009. A study by Entertainment Media Research in the UK found that 71 per cent of those who admitted they increased their file-sharing activity in 2008 did so "because it's free". In Norway, research by Norstat in 2009 also found the most-cited reason for illegal downloading from P2P services was "because it's free". Further studies came to broadly the same conclusion in Japan and Belgium in 2009 (IFPI).

It is the "free-to-user" appeal of illegal file-sharing that creates its unfair advantage over legitimate music services, whose cost base, including payments to artists and copyright holders, cannot compete with the free illegal alternative. This, more than any other factor, explains why the growth of an innovative and entrepreneurial legitimate music sector is being stunted in the absence of an effective response to digital piracy.

The Impact on Local Talent

Illegal file-sharing has also had a very significant, and sometimes disastrous, impact on investment in artists and local repertoire. With their revenues eroded by piracy, music companies have far less to plough back into local artist development. Much has been made of the idea that growing live music revenues can compensate for the fall-off in recorded music sales, but this is, in reality, a myth.

Live performance earnings are generally more to the benefit of veteran, established acts, while it is the younger, developing acts, without lucrative live careers, who do not have the chance to develop their reputation through recorded music sales.

Clear evidence of this impact can be seen in markets including France, Spain and Brazil.

- In France, there has been a striking fall in the number of local repertoire albums released in recent years. In the first half of 2009, 107 French-repertoire albums were released, 60 per cent down on the 271 in the same period of 2003. French artist signings have also slumped by 60 per cent, from 91 in the first half of 2002 to 35 in the same period of 2009. Overall investment in marketing and promotion by the French music industry fell nine per cent in the first six months of 2009. It is estimated that 25 per cent of the French internet population currently download music illegally from P2P networks or other sources on a monthly basis (Jupiter Research, 2009).
- In Spain, a culture of state-tolerated apathy towards illegal file-sharing has contributed to a dramatic slump in the music market. Spain has the worst online piracy problem of any major market in Europe. Today, P2P usage in Spain, at 32 per cent of internet users, is more than double the European rate of 15 per cent (Jupiter Research, 2009).
- The Spanish legitimate music market is now only one third of its size in 2001 and fell by around 17 per cent in 2009 alone. Local artist album sales in the Top 50 declined by 65 per cent between 2004 and 2009.
- In Brazil, music sales fell by more than 40 per cent between 2005 and 2009, with a disastrous impact on invest-

---

**Percentage of Active Internet Users
Who Access Unlicensed Services**

Brazil	44%
EU Top 5 Markets	23%
Spain	45%

Active Internet users are monthly users of the Internet. Unlicensed services are selected P2P [peer-to-peer] and non-P2P services used to access various content, including music.

TAKEN FROM: IFPI, "IFPI Digital Report 2011," 2011, p. 14. www.ifpi .org/content/library/DMR2011.pdf.

---

ment in local repertoire. In 2008 there were only 67 full-priced local artist album releases by the five biggest music companies in Brazil—just one tenth of the number (625) a decade earlier. This has been particularly damaging in a market where 70 per cent of music consumed is domestic repertoire. . . .

Impact on the Creative Sector

For years digital piracy has been a problem most associated with music. Today, however, creative industries including movie, publishing and television, regard "monetising" the online world and addressing digital piracy as their greatest challenges.

"The music industry was hit first, but now with increased broadband you have a situation where all the creative industries are at a tipping point," says Simon Renshaw, Los Angeles–based manager of a long list of major artists including the Dixie Chicks. "You can see it in the collapsing DVD market; you can see what's going on in TV, newspapers and magazines. And now we're seeing the same thing in the book publishing business and you're going to start seeing piracy of novels and reference books." Renshaw passionately believes that the stakes involved go far wider than the music industry. "What I worry about is that we are heading into a world where copyright has no value and where there's no incentive for anyone to provide patronage and support for the creators of intellectual property."

He says the world has transformed, for both young and established artists and the economy of jobs and activity that surround them. "We're dealing with this every week—everything that you can afford to do around a record is greatly reduced and that also means that everything that you're spending with video companies, with hotels, with airlines, with graphic artists, makeup—everything's reduced, maybe by 70 per cent. The money is not there anymore. And if there are no rock stars the whole industry and the people working in it suffer."

> *"If I give any of [my property rights] up, all of a sudden, composing music (i.e., making Art) is my hobby, and I have to make my living outside of it."*

Copyright Helps Artists Make a Living

Jonathan Newman

Jonathan Newman is a classical, or concert, music composer. In the following viewpoint, he argues that exploiting copyright is how he manages to make a living as a composer and self-publisher. He says that without the rights granted to him by copyright protection, music would have to be his hobby rather than his profession. He notes that those who recommend doing away with copyright have not managed to explain how artists would make a living without it. He concludes that in a capitalist society, it is both fair and necessary to pay artists for their art.

As you read, consider the following questions:

1. What rights does Newman say the composer has once he or she has created a piece of music?
2. What content does the author say he gives away for free on his website?

3. According to Newman, what problems can composers run into when they try to set poems to music?

I am a composer of what we (or at least other composers) tend to call "Concert Music", that is, music for string quartets and orchestras and choruses and other things where you sit quietly in a darkened hall while shooting dirty looks at the old lady unwrapping a cough drop. I am expensively and elitistly-trained, and work (mostly) by commission. It is pretentious, it is fun, and I do it professionally. . . .

Copyright and Self-Publishing

I've noticed more than a little talk about copyright essentially being created for and serving only the Publisher, and not the Creator. But what if that's the same person? Save one or two works, I am a self-published composer; I run my own "publishing company" (it's not, really, it's just me and my Schedule C [a tax form for self-employment] and a quirky company name), but while serving that function I do all the things a traditional publisher would do, including its main function: to exploit the copyrights it owns. Doing this myself pretty much avoids exactly what Nina Paley [a film-maker and advocate of free culture] describes as the "gate-keepers"—those faceless corporate intellectual copyright owners who keep The Artist down. But I *am* the Artist (and the Publisher, the two are halves of each other in the case of copyright), and so even though "exploit" isn't exactly a friendly word, it works fine, because there are in fact multiple ways to make a property (a piece of art) work for both. Because for me, owning my works, and controlling their distribution through licensing, is how I'm able to survive as a working composer.

Most people don't realize that when you make a work—and I'll use music as an example for obvious reasons—your rights concerning the piece are numerous, and on several levels. I'm probably missing one or two, but once your new hypothetical work is completed (Congratulations, writing music is hard) you're faced with what is actually a constellation of rights, all of which one, or his/her evil representative if s/he's traditionally-published, can "exploit":

- The right to reproduce it (make photocopies, bound copies, whatever)
- The right to publish and distribute it (these days you should think twice before signing that one away)
- The right to sync it to [a] motion-picture (this was the prickly one for Nina Paley [who had trouble obtaining rights to the music for her film *Sita Sings the Blues*])
- The right to "grand" staging (use in a play or ballet or pretty much anything else with costumes)
- The right to record it (the first time that is, and then anyone can do it as long as they pay the statutory mechanical rates. Thus, covers.)
- The right to "prepare derivative works" from it (for music that usually means arrange it for other ensembles or instrumentations. For books and whatnot that usually means licensing the rights for the opera, or the movie)
- The right to broadcast it (radio)
- and the right to perform it (the biggie)

Making a Middle-Class Living

Now, which one of these would you like me to ignore because you have a yen to use my piece for your own art? My performing rights royalties alone (collected for me by my Performing Rights Agency Of Choice, ASCAP, which also collects any broadcast royalties that might happen) are actually a significant chunk of my income. Does Free Culture [a movement that argues for the abolition, or drastic reduction, of copyright] want to perform my piece without my collecting that? It might help to know that performing rights royalties are split 50/50 between writer and the publisher. As my own publisher, I receive 100% of them. (Another gate jumped.)

What about when someone likes my recent chorus piece, and wants to arrange it for their brass choir? I should have an open-source attitude [that is, allow others to use it for free], right? Forget the arranging license (and the fee that goes with it) and let everyone have it, because it's good for creativity and good for artists?

My point is that any one of these singly isn't such a big deal, and I'm all for the big picture of helping the Cause of Creativity. But taken as a whole, managing the above list becomes this precious bundle of life-giving manna—if you're interested in being a composer making a middle-class living that is. Which I am. I don't teach professionally (only occasionally, usually as a guest artist at a university), so if I give *any* of these up, all of a sudden, composing music (i.e., making Art) is my *hobby*, and I have to make my living outside of it. And I've found that the people most vocal about the benefits of free culture, or maybe most lax in shepherding the above rights, are those who choose to make their living some other way.

When asked in [an] interview the other day, Nina Paley replied to a question about Free Culture creating "a situation where you can't have an artistic middle class.":

> What we have now is you can get paid for craft. You don't get paid for art. You get paid for craft. Every animator that I know, or almost every animator that I know, works at a studio, working on shit. They know it's shit. They do their best to not think about it, but it's god-awful commercial shit.

Actually, I get paid for Art. I *could* have chosen to get paid for craft (being an orchestrator, or a commercial music writer) and decided I was actually *better* at making Art. And it's a slog, let me tell you, selling Art. Because Art is, I'm sure you all noticed, incredibly subjective. Only a few out of many like my stuff, and even less love it (shocking, I know). If I expected many to like it, I'd be writing very different music, and would have a lot more wiggle room when it came to giving away my stuff for the sake of Art.

Paley also talked about art not being a profession:

No, I wanted to keep it pure, the love of the craft. When I was quitting *Fluff* [Paley's comic strip], I said "make art not money, make art not money. Remember that." And of course I forget periodically and get confused and think that I should be making money and not art. They're not mutually exclusive, not at all; but you've got to remember: don't do stuff that's bad for your soul in order to make money.

Art *and* Money

I realize how mercenary this sounds, but how about making art *and* money? Ultimately I'm unclear how copyleft [using copyright to make it easier to distribute copies and modified versions of a work] (or free culture in general) can maintain my middle-class income. As far as I can tell, the current copyright laws are what do that.

All that being said, I'm actually a fan of Free. I give away content like crazy on my website—mp3 downloads—scores of the pieces as PDFs, etc. I give away CDs, even commercial ones, like candy. I give away *many* (expensive to produce) printed scores. Because I do believe that giving away significant content—not just useless crap, but stuff people can use—in many ways does help create that "fan base" one hears the astute bands and rock stars talk about—those fans that downloaded the album for free, but who later on shell out 300 bucks to go to the tour show and buy the $25 t-shirts. Which right there crystallizes the line for the Free argument. You don't see "Pay what you want" Radiohead (I'm a fan) letting their devoted following into the show for free. (Or do you? I don't really know.)

So among this noise, *some* content is always controlled by the owner. It's not all free, it's just a question of *what* content is deemed not free. For me, it's the performance materials. That's the paper (maybe someday it won't be, I'm looking at you, iPads) musicians rehearse and perform from. I rent it, I sell it, I control it. Nothing drives me more bat-shit crazy than seeing other composers give away their stuff. A website full of scores and parts—"Come play my music! I won't charge! I just want you to play it to Get My Name Out There!" Well, a) I hope you have another job, b) you just made mine a lot harder, and c) the end user (who, sure, now knows your name) thinks your stuff isn't even worth the paper it's printed on.

Paley giving away her (beautiful) movie is great and all, but I can't exactly sell "Jonathan Newman" t-shirts to make up the difference. If all the cool kids started wearing Sita pins and she turned into a pop culture icon, then it hardly matters whether anyone paid to show the film. As much as I've tried to make it one, that avenue is not really an option for me.

It's true, 70 years after death [US copyrights last for seventy years from the creator's death] *is* a silly amount. 50 did seem like enough—2 generations after death ("My Granddaddy made that! You can't touch it!")—does seem like enough time for the family to come up with some more original content, but, as we all know, Disney had other ideas [Disney helped push a copyright extension through Congress to make sure Mickey Mouse did not fall out of copyright]. Still, before these protections, composers *did* have to scramble. In 1945 [composer Igor] Stravinsky famously changed all the half notes to quarter notes in [his suite] *Firebird* (not really, but you get the idea) to make a newly copyrightable version for the U.S, so he could prevent the loss of income from performances there. Nothing new under the sun.

Exploit the Copyright

I feel Paley's pain, dealing with copyright owners. Just ask any composer about getting text permission from a publisher for a poem he or she wants to set [to music]. Try figuring out who owns the poem in the first place. Or if it's PD [in the public domain; that is, out of copyright] or not. I've actually been working on an opera for the last couple of years. The first year of it was just figuring out who actually *owned* the film my collaborator and I wanted to adapt. I see the problem as not necessarily the rules themselves, but the companies/businesses/corporations who collect the intellectual property and then seem to want to hoard it without licensing it, simply because it doesn't seem worth it to expend the time/energy/resources/employees to [make the] deal. Their mistake is that it is very much worth it. Exploiting the copyright (issuing licenses and collecting the fees), is the entire point of owning the property, whether it's small or not. When they do that, they are serving the Publisher function. It's *how* or whether they'll do it at all that's causing problems.

And so, I'm finding the Free Culture argument suspect. If someone wanted to copy my bicycle so that there's now "one for each of us", my honest reaction would probably be 'F--- you. I spent 3 years making that bicycle. Make your own damn bicycle.' Not exactly a constructive argument, granted, but let's at least acknowledge that we're not talking about a bicycle. Bicycles are not special. They are not (generally) art. Yeeesss, all art is derivative, it's true. Art is synthesis, and some synthesis is better (brilliant, "original") than others. But creativity cannot be its own reward. We still live in, for better and often worse, a capitalist society, and in *no* other profession in that society is a lack of compensation expected, like it is with Art. People get paid for *charity work*, for goodness sakes. At some point, someone, has to charge someone else, something.

| "The majority of the artists are not convinced that file-sharing is doing them any financial harm."

Copyright Violations Do Not Hurt Artists' Income

Ernesto Van Der Sar

Ernesto Van Der Sar is the pseudonym of the founder and editor in chief of TorrentFreak, a file-sharing news website. In the following viewpoint, Van Der Sar reports on a Dutch study about artist attitudes to file sharing. The study concluded that a majority of artists believed that file sharing did not hurt their income but instead helped spread the word about their music. The survey also showed that many artists themselves downloaded music illegally. The survey said that artists felt that downloaders should be punished, but Van Der Sar nonetheless felt the study showed that artists were becoming more accepting of file sharing.

As you read, consider the following questions:

1. According to the survey cited by the author, what percentage of artists themselves download files illegally?
2. Are highly educated artists more or less favorable to file sharing, according to the survey cited by Van Der Sar?

3. What attitudes does the survey cited by the author show that artists have toward DRM?

When anti-piracy outfits and Big Media speak out against file-sharing they often claim to be standing up for the interests of the artists. However, a new survey among nearly 4,000 artists has revealed that nearly a quarter are pirating the works of fellow artists. Contrary to popular belief among higher level execs in the entertainment industry, the younger generation of artists believe that file-sharing helps them to gain an audience.

Artists Are Pirates, Too

Yesterday [April 11, 2011], the Dutch Government announced plans to outlaw downloading of all copyrighted material and measures to make it easier to block websites that facilitate copyright infringement. An interesting move, particularly since a survey they published on the same day shows that artists' views on file-sharing are not all that negative.

Through an elaborate survey the Government wanted to find out more about the views of artists on piracy, DRM [digital rights management: technologies that limit access to digital content], and other opportunities and challenges they face in the digital era. The questions covered in this article were answered by nearly 4,000 artists of all ages, including musicians, filmmakers, authors and photographers. The results give a unique insight into the position of artists on this controversial subject.

One of the results that stands out directly is that artists are pirates too. Not all of them of course, but a healthy percentage. Of all the respondents surveyed on the subject, 22% indicated that they had downloaded copyrighted works without the owners' permission in the last 12 months. Another 71% told the researchers they hadn't downloaded anything without permission during this period, and the remaining 7% didn't know, or didn't want to answer the question.

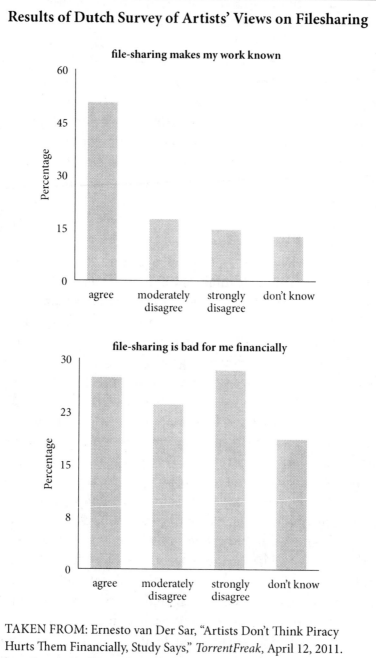

Results of Dutch Survey of Artists' Views on Filesharing

file-sharing makes my work known

file-sharing is bad for me financially

TAKEN FROM: Ernesto van Der Sar, "Artists Don't Think Piracy Hurts Them Financially, Study Says," *TorrentFreak*, April 12, 2011. http://torrentfreak.com.

A follow up question among those who admitted to downloading others' copyrighted works, found that music is by far the most downloaded media type. Over 80% of the downloaders downloaded music, and little over 40% also downloaded movies. Other categories such as E-books and games were less popular, with around 5% downloaders interested in these works.

Aside from their own 'piracy' habits, the survey also asked the respondents about their role as 'victims' of unauthorized file-sharing.

File-Sharing Helps Artists

One of the questions dealt with whether the artists think they are being financially harmed by file-sharing. Interestingly, only about 12% of artists completely agree with the statement that file-sharing hurts them ($\approx$16% agree). The majority of the artists are not convinced that file-sharing is doing them any financial harm, and some actually think the opposite is true. What's worth noting is that higher educated artists in particular believe that file-sharing is doing them no financial harm.

Instead of hurting their wallets, the majority of the artists believe that file-sharing helps to promote their work. Little over 50% of those questioned responded affirmatively to the question of whether file-sharing helps to get their work known among the public, while only 5% completely disagreed with this statement. In particular the younger artists (< 25yo) recognized promotional benefits, as more than 80% thought file-sharing increases the popularity of their work.

Moving on to DRM, the survey found that 30% of the artists believe that DRM is hurting legitimate customers through access restrictions. Despite this negative view, 70% of all artists still believe their work should be protected by DRM. With regard to DRM there appears to be quite a large generation gap. More than 40% of the artists younger than 25 years old say DRM is hurting their relationship with the public, while none of the artists over 75 years old believes it does any harm.

Finally, the artists were also surveyed on whether individual file-sharers should be treated more harshly. Interestingly, close to 60% indicate that they should, with an even higher percentage among the older artists. Even among the people who admitted that they were downloading without permission, nearly one third said that harsher measures are needed to deter file-sharers.

All in all it can be concluded from the survey that the majority of Dutch artists don't believe that unauthorized file-sharing is hurting them financially, and that it may actually help them to gain a larger audience. Despite these liberal views, a majority of the artists support harsher measures against unauthorized file-sharing and for DRM to 'protect' their works.

A mixed message, but one that's hopeful, especially since the younger generations recognize the benefits of sharing, even when it's without permission.

Periodical and Internet Sources Bibliography

The following articles have been selected to supplement the diverse views presented in this chapter.

Paul Connolly	"Do You Download Music Illegally? Congratulations, You Are Killing the UK Pop Industry," *Daily Mail* (London), March 25, 2010.
Contrapuntist	"Copyright Dilemma, the Internet, and the Music Industry vs. the People," February 19, 2009. www.thecontrapuntist.com.
Kevin Goldberg	"White House on Copyright: PRA, Yes! Illegal Streaming, No!," CommLawBlog, March 17, 2011. www.commlawblog.com.
Mike Masnick	"For Lady Gaga, Copyright Not About Music, but Her Image," TechDirt, March 9, 2011. www.techdirt.com.
NPR Online	"Digital Music Sampling: Creativity or Criminality?," January 28, 2011. www.npr.org.
Darren Ressler	"Kevin Saunderson Fights Unauthorized Sampling of 'The Sound' by Giving the Track Away," *Big Shot*, February 21, 2011.
Amir Said	"RIAA 'Bloodbath' Clears Way for Sampling," Blame the Critic blog, March 5, 2009. www.blamethecritic.com.
Ben Sheffner	"Songwriters Guild's Carnes on Piracy and 'Cyber-Somalia,'" Copyrights & Campaigns blog, January 30, 2009. http://copyrightsandcampaigns.blogspot.com.
Sonic Fiction	"Pop Ate Itself," November 11, 2010. http://sonicfictionjourno.wordpress.com.

CHAPTER 2

How Should the Music Industry Respond to the Changing Market?

Chapter Preface

The CD, or compact disc, uses laser technology to store digital data. CDs were developed by the Dutch electronics company Phillips. Research into creating laser audio discs began in the 1970s, and intensified at Phillips in 1977. In 1979, Phillips partnered with Sony to further develop the disc. "Sony insisted that a disc must hold all of Beethoven's 9th Symphony," according to an August 17, 2007, article at BBC Online. This established the standard size of CDs; 12cm in diameter, able to hold about 74 minutes of music. Phillips and Sony produced a "Red Book" in 1980 which "outlined the specifications regarding CD Digital Audio," according to a January 28, 2003, article on the website Molecular Expressions. The standardization helped to encourage the growth of CDs as a widely used format.

The first commercial CDs were produced in 1982; they were Abba's *The Visitor* and Herbert von Karajan conducting Richard Strauss's *Alpine* Symphony. In 1985, according to an article titled "History of the Compact Disc" at Discmakers, "Dire Straits' *Brothers in Arms* became the first CD to sell more than one million copies."

Though record companies were hesitant to embrace the technology at first, CDs quickly became a huge bonanza for the record industry. According to Robert Sandall, writing for *Prospect* on August 1, 2007, "The compact disc ushered in the biggest boom in profits the record companies had known since 7" singles gave way to 12" LPs in the late 1960s. The CD persuaded many music fans to replace their vinyl collection with digital copies of music they had already paid for. And the rise of the CD permitted record companies to double the price of their basic product without incurring a huge uplift in costs. Even allowing for the royalty paid to the joint inventors of the CD—Philips and Sony—the discs were soon being manufactured for little more than it cost to crank out vinyl records on ancient presses."

However, as Sandall notes, "the CD contained the seeds of its own destruction." Once music was stored digitally, it could be reproduced without a loss of quality. As home computers became common and technology advanced, it became easy to burn multiple perfect copies of the same music. This culminated in digital music files available online—often illegally—for free. CD sales peaked in 2000, and have been dropping since. Their heydey as an audio format appears to have passed.

The following viewpoints look at how musicians are trying to generate revenue in light of the changes epitomized by the fall of the compact disc.

> *"Things are not going to get better for CD sales unless the price point is addressed."*

Lower CD Prices May Increase Sales

Ed Christman

Ed Christman is a music industry journalist and a senior correspondent for Billboard. *In the following viewpoint, he reports that Universal Music Group, one of the major music labels, is planning to lower the price of its CDs. The CD prices should come down to between six and ten dollars, Christman says. Christman reports that retailers are generally enthusiastic about the change and hope that it will reverse the slump in CD sales.*

As you read, consider the following questions:

1. According to Christman, how does UMG hope to offset the loss in revenue per CD?
2. Why does the author say retailer enthusiasm for the program may be tempered?
3. What was the JumpStart pricing program, according to Christman?

Universal Music Group (UMG) is embarking on one of the most ambitious efforts yet to boost U.S. CD sales, with the test of a new pricing structure designed to sell most new releases by current artists at $10 or less at retail.

New Life

The major's "Velocity" pricing program responds to the continuing plunge in CD sales, taking aim at brick-and-mortar retail stores that have scaled back on floor space dedicated to music. The pricing adjustments will also bring CD prices more in line with what consumers pay for digital albums at online retailers like iTunes and Amazon.

"We think it will really bring new life into the physical format," Universal Music Group Distribution chairman/CEO Jim Urie says.

Universal, which accounts for 28.7 percent of year-to-date [2010] U.S. album sales, according to [research organization] Nielsen SoundScan, will cut UMG's main wholesale price point of $10.35 to about $7.50 or less for front-line releases, which are generally by established current artists. It's also breaking with prevailing industry practice by putting suggested retail prices on CDs, ranging from $6 to $10.

UMG is betting that it can offset the loss in revenue per CD with increased sales volume and the rollout of greater numbers of higher-priced, higher-margin deluxe editions of albums. The new CD pricing structure could also spur UMG imprints to find ways to reduce CD costs, such as embracing less elaborate packaging on standard single CD releases or placing fewer songs on albums in order to reduce mechanical royalty payments to songwriters.

Most new releases will carry the new price points, although there will be the occasional exception, UMG sources say. The Velocity program will begin in the second quarter [of 2010] and run through most of the year. Sources say the first titles to be released under Velocity are expected to include new albums by Godsmack, Game and Taio Cruz.

Retail Reaction

Retailers should respond well to the new price points, given that many of them were already pricing many new releases at $10 and absorbing the loss to generate foot traffic to their stores.

But their enthusiasm may be tempered by the narrower profit margins expected under the new pricing structure. According to sources, front-line UMG releases will carry a 25 percent profit margin, down sharply from the customary 35 percent. That means CDs with a suggested list price of $10 would wholesale for $7.50, those with a $9 list for $6.75 and so on.

The move may not go over well with retailers that buy from wholesalers and already reap a narrower margin than those that buy direct from labels. And merchants accustomed to having free rein in setting retail prices may chafe at the suggested list prices. Meanwhile, UMG artists and their managers may grumble about the pricing initiative, since royalty payments, usually a percentage of sales, will be calculated based on the lower price points.

"We are happy to see that a major music vendor has made a decision to lower its price substantially," Bob Higgins, chairman/CEO of retail operator Trans World Entertainment, says, "because it's what the customer wants today, and (because lower pricing is needed) if we are going to see a viable CD business continue."

Similarly, Newbury Comics CEO Mike Dreese says he gives the initiative "two thumbs up," but adds that the industry still needs the other major labels and independents to make similar reductions in front-line pricing to boost overall CD sales.

Merchants have long clamored that lower pricing alone would prolong the life of the CD, sales of which are down 15.4 percent in the United States so far this year [March 2010] from the same period in 2009, according to SoundScan. With retail Sunday circulars and the home page of Apple's iTunes store touting hit titles at $9.99, it became conventional wisdom among merchants that $10 was the magic price point that would induce consumers to buy more CDs.

UMG was the first major to cut wholesale CD prices when it initiated its JumpStart pricing program in 2003. The other majors initially condemned the move, but eventually began reducing prices on their own catalog titles. Such initiatives have brought wholesale prices down to the $6–$8 range for midline and full-priced titles. Front-line pricing, however, remains a mixed bag, with UMG's main wholesale price point at $10.35, Sony's at $10.50, EMI's at $12.04, and Warner Music Group's at $12.05.

Last year [2009], Trans World enlisted the participation of UMG, Sony and EMI in a pricing experiment to sell every CD for $9.99, an initiative that it has extended to more than 100 of its stores.

"Things are not going to get better for CD sales unless the price point is addressed," a senior retail executive says. "One thing that the Trans World test shows for sure: $10 will drive sales and traffic."

> *"Whatever advantages [CDs] may*
> *have offered in 1983, they're a crap*
> *format now."*

The CD Format Should Be Dropped

Miles Raymer

Miles Raymer is a music writer for the Chicago Reader. *In the following viewpoint he argues that the CD will shortly be extinct. He says that CD sound quality is no better than digital, and that vinyl records provide better packaging for those interested in collecting. He reports that several Chicago independent labels are moving away from the CD format. Instead of CDs, he says, they are choosing to release music only digitally, or digitally and on collectible vinyl.*

As you read, consider the following questions:

1. What does Raymer say is the only defensible reason to buy a CD?
2. What are the two camps of CD consumers, according to James Kenler, as cited by the author?
3. According to Bruce Adams, as cited by Raymer, what are two reasons for independent labels to give up on CDs?

Miles Raymer, "Sharp Darts: Format Wars!" *Chicago Reader*, April 24, 2008. Reproduced by permission.

In 1987 Big Black released a CD compilation called *The Rich Man's Eight Track Tape* with the following admonition printed on the face of the disc: "When, in five years, this remarkable achievement in the advancement of fidelity is obsolete and unplayable on any 'modern' equipment, remember, in 1971, the 8-track tape was the state of the art." Though CDs have hardly gone the way of the eight-track, it's hard to argue that they've earned their longevity—whatever advantages they may have offered in 1983, they're a crap format now.

Music as Artifact

Given that my speakers and headphones—like most people's gear, I bet—sound just as good playing 192 kbps MP3s as they do playing CDs, there's no good reason for me to have heaps of jewel cases and Digipaks on my shelves, in my cabinets, stacked on top of my cabinets, and spilling across my desk. Even at the same bit rate as CDs, sound files are way handier—easier to store, easier to send, easier to copy. They don't fill up my personal space with disposable plastic crap, and they're not made from bisphenol-A [an environmentally unfriendly kind of plastic].

The only defensible reason to buy CDs these days is an attachment to music-as-artifact—every so often you see one with really beautiful packaging. But on that front they lose out big to vinyl, which offers album artists a much bigger canvas and sidesteps the annoying problem of fragile jewel cases and CD spindles. If you're going to own music you have to lug around, vinyl is the obvious choice—even if you don't respond to LPs as totemic objects, like so many record fiends do, you have to admit that their creamy analog sound beats the hell out of digital reproductions. (That's right, I said it.) CDs don't do nearly as much to justify the physical space they require.

I'm probably more fed up with CDs than the average person because they're part of my job. In fact the only people I know who are as tired of CDs as I am are running record labels. Though advances in computer and Internet technology rendered the format obsolete almost a decade ago, only now is its passing really starting to look inevitable—the majors have been complaining about sagging CD sales for years, of course, and when I talked to [independent labels] Drag City, Thrill Jockey, and Flameshovel for this story, they confirmed that they've experienced similar drops. But all three labels also report steady increases in sales of digital downloads and vinyl. Those trends seem to suggest a pretty clear business plan, at least for the near-term future, and two local imprints are already on board.

No More CDs

This week Flameshovel is putting out Make Believe's *Going to the Bone Church* as a vinyl LP and an unlocked MP3 download—it's the label's first release that won't have a CD version at all. This, according to Flameshovel cohead James Kenler, is the way his label might end up releasing everything. One camp of consumers, he says, "doesn't see any innate value in consumable music at this point. So these people steal music, rip from their friends' CDs, or don't really have any strong feelings about the aesthetics of the CDs they do purchase." He admits that this is a generalization, but it fits more than a few people I know who own huge hard drives full of music and haven't bought a CD since Napster [a file-sharing site established in 1999] happened. "The other extreme," he says, "is that you have someone who cares to the utmost level about the packaging, and they're the ones who are going to continue to buy music no matter how they do it, and they're interested in a more tangible connection." Kenler's strategy is to cater more to that second set and worry less about people who wouldn't be giving him money anyway.

Make Believe fans willing to pay for that tangible connection will get a collectible 180-gram LP and a poster in a sleeve of high-quality stock; the album's being pressed in an edition of 1,000 (450 copies bone colored), and Kenler says any future pressings will be in different packaging so as not to dilute the collectibility of this edition. Plus every record comes with a download code.

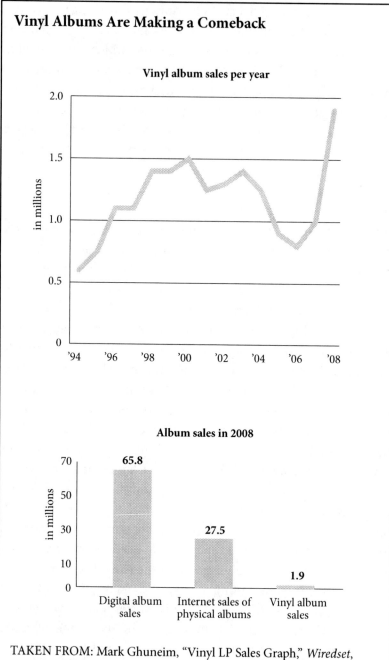

Vinyl Albums Are Making a Comeback

Vinyl album sales per year

Album sales in 2008

TAKEN FROM: Mark Ghuneim, "Vinyl LP Sales Graph," *Wiredset*, April 27, 2009. www.wiredset.com.

"People who don't have record players or are concerned about the portability of LPs," he says, "can still download it directly from our site and have it for their iPods and their cars."

"In a lot of ways this is a test," Kenler explains. "Some of the other people in the industry we've talked about it with are interested to see how it pans out for us. . . . I don't know that it means we'll be doing more releases just vinyl and digitally, or if it means we're going to try to play up this sort of polarized market we're looking at. Even with CDs, do we make them more limited in scope, more aesthetically pleasing, spend a little more money on packaging and charge a little more for it for the people who want to buy it, and spend less and concern ourselves less with hitting the broader market?"

Bruce Adams, cofounder of [the label] Kranky, seems a little more confident about what direction to take. His new label, Flingco Sound System [FSS](he sold his share of Kranky in 2005), won't be selling CDs at all, just album downloads and vinyl. "Rather than invest money in printing CDs," he says, "I decided to invest in the capacity to sell downloads myself. The onetime investment in software coding will generate returns for a long time. The profit margin on a download album is healthy, too."

More Room in the Basement

FSS plans to put out four albums its first year, two of them digitally and two as digital-vinyl combos. Like *Bone Church*, FSS's vinyl pressings are aimed at connoisseurs—Adams believes the "buying physical artifacts" market is shifting toward that customer base. "Record stores are dwindling in number," he says. "Those that are left in five years might be more like [vintage record stores] Aquarius Records [in San Francisco] or Dusty Groove [in Chicago] than Tower Records [a retail chain that closed in 2006]. They will want unique products to draw customers through the door."

It helps that the extremely uncommercial artists on FSS's release schedule appeal pretty much exclusively to an audience that takes its music seriously—not too many trend hoppers will be checking out the gnarly melted-down black metal of Wrnlrd or the eerie electroacoustic experiments of Haptic. Adams hopes to earn the loyalty of that audience with a subscription service that rewards them with goodies like nonalbum music and posters. "The big advantage in the model that I see," says Adams, "is the opportunity to have a direct relationship with customers. I can send music directly to them digitally; I can offer special bonus items (both physical and digital) that they can't get anywhere else."

Adams doesn't see how self-financed start-up labels have any incentive to mass-produce CDs anymore—sinking $5,000 into a run, he says, "seems like a losing bet for anyone putting their own money on the line." But that's not the only reason he's ditching the format. "Cutting out CDs," he says, "means more room in my basement."

"Music isn't going away. We're just moving out of the brief period . . . when an artist could expect to make a living selling records alone."

The New Rock-Star Paradigm

Damian Kulash Jr.

Damian Kulash Jr. is the lead singer of the rock band OK Go. In the following viewpoint, he argues that selling albums is becoming less and less important for musicians. He says that the old model of creating CDs on a record label is being replaced by many other revenue streams, including corporate sponsorship and merchandise. Kulash concludes that musicians are selling themselves and their personal relationship with their fans that can be measured through Twitter feeds, Facebook friends, YouTube views, and other online metrics.

As you read, consider the following questions:

1. What evidence does Kulash provide that the CD business is imploding with increasing vigor?
2. According to the author, what evidence is there that touring is not replacing CD sales for most acts?

Damian Kulash Jr., "The New Rock-Star Paradigm," *Wall Street Journal*, December 17, 2010. Reprinted by permission of *The Wall Street Journal*. Copyright © 2010 Dow Jones & Company, Inc. All rights reserved worldwide. License number 2790280150838.

3. Why does Kulash say that corporate sponsorship is not of much use to starting acts?

Succeeding in the music business isn't just about selling albums anymore. The lead singer of OK Go on how to make it without a record label (treadmill videos help)

My rock band has leapt across treadmills, camouflaged ourselves in wallpaper, performed with the Notre Dame marching band, danced with a dozen trained dogs, made an animation with 2,300 pieces of toast, crammed a day-long continuous shot into 4½ minutes and built the first ever Rube Goldberg machine—at least that we know of—to operate in time to music. We are known for our music videos, which we make with the same passion and perseverance we do our songs. Our videos have combined views in excess of 120 million on YouTube alone, with countless millions more from television and repostings all over the Internet.

For most people, the obvious question is: Has this helped sell records? The quick answer is yes. We've sold more than 600,000 records over the last decade. But the more relevant answer is that doesn't really matter. A half a million records is nothing to shake a stick at, but it's the online statistics that set the tone of our business and, ultimately, the size of our income.

We once relied on investment and support from a major label. Now we make a comparable living raising money directly from fans and through licensing and sponsorship. Our bank accounts don't rival Lady Gaga's, but we've got more creative freedom than we did as small fish in her pond.

For a decade, analysts have been hyperventilating about the demise of the music industry. But music isn't going away. We're just moving out of the brief period—a flash in history's pan—when an artist could expect to make a living selling records alone. Music is as old as humanity itself, and just as difficult to define. It's an ephemeral, temporal and subjective experience.

For several decades, though, from about World War II until sometime in the last 10 years, the recording industry managed to successfully and profitably pin it down to a stable, if circular, definition: Music was recordings of music. Records not only made it possible for musicians to connect with listeners anywhere, at any time, but offered a discrete package for commoditization. It was the perfect bottling of lightning: A powerful experience could be packaged in plastic and then bought and sold like any other commercial product.

Then came the Internet, and in less than a decade, that system fell. With uncontrollable and infinite duplication and distribution of recordings, selling records suddenly became a lot like selling apples to people who live in orchards. In 1999, global record sales totaled $26.9 billion; in 2009, that figure, including digital purchases, which now represent 25% of sales (nearly 50% in the U.S.), is down to $17 billion. For eight of the last 10 years, the decline in revenue from record sales has gotten steeper, which is to say the business is imploding with increasing vigor.

Music is getting harder to define again. It's becoming more of an experience and less of an object. Without records as clearly delineated receptacles of value, last century's rules—both industrial and creative—are out the window. For those who can find an audience or a paycheck outside the traditional system, this can mean blessed freedom from the music industry's gatekeepers.

Georgia singer/songwriter Corey Smith has never had a traditional record contract, but in 2008 he grossed about $4 million from touring, merchandise and other revenue, yielding roughly $2 million that was reinvested in the singer's business, according to his manager, Marty Winsch. Mr. Smith makes his recordings downloadable at no cost from his website, and Mr. Winsch emphasizes that they are promotion for his live shows, not the other way around. "We don't look at it as 'free,'" he says. "When people come to the website and download the music, they're giving us their time, their most valuable commodity." Recently, Mr. Smith entered a partnership with a small music company, but unlike a traditional label deal, the arrangement will give him 50% of any net revenue.

Mr. Smith's touring success, unfortunately, isn't indicative of industry trends. Live performance, once seen as the last great hope of the music industry, now looks like anything but. Live Nation, the largest concert promoter in the U.S., recently reported that concert revenue is down 14.5% since last year. A report by Edison Research found that in 2010, 12-to-24-year-olds went to fewer than half as many concerts as they did in 2000; nearly two-thirds went to none at all.

So if vanishing record revenue isn't being replaced by touring income, how are musicians feeding themselves? For moderately well established artists, the answer is increasingly corporate sponsorship and licensing—a return, in a sense, to the centuries-old logic of patronage. In 1995, it was rare for musicians to partner with corporations; in most corners of the music industry, it was seen as the ultimate sell-out. But with investments from labels harder to come by, attitudes towards outside corporate deals have changed.

These days, money coming from a record label often comes with more embedded creative restrictions than the marketing dollars of other industries. A record label typically measures success in number of records sold. Outside sponsors, by contrast, tend to take a broader view of success. The measuring stick could be mentions in the press, traffic to a website, email addresses collected or views of online videos. Artists have meaningful, direct, and emotional access to our fans, and at a time when capturing the public's attention is increasingly difficult for the army of competing marketers, that access is a big asset.

My band parted ways with the record label EMI a little less than a year ago. While we were profitable for them, our margins were smaller than those of more traditionally successful bands, because our YouTube views don't directly generate as much revenue as record sales. Our idea of what constitutes success and

The Spread of Music Videos

Music videos have started showing up in forms that belie the confusion of music video (as a form) and music television (as a delivery technology for that form): music videos now come to us on DVDs and enhanced CDs; on PDAs, cell phones, and other wireless communication devices; and perhaps most importantly, on the Internet. In this new millennium nearly every band seems to have a Web site, and vast numbers of these sites are home to music videos. Every record label—from indies like K Records and Matador to the music arms of multinational corporations like Arista—features videos on its site, where they almost always are promoted on the front pages. And MTV has gotten into the act, too, with its high traffic Web site featuring literally thousands of video clips. There are dozens upon dozens of other sites—including Launch.com (now part of Yahoo!), sonicnet.com (now owned by Viacom and branded by VH1), and Rollingstone.com—that offer access to music videos in which a model is used similar to the MTV online model with videos as part of a broad array of music information.

Roger Beebe and Jason Middleton, eds.,
Medium Cool: Music Videos from Soundies
to Cellphones, *2007.*

how to wring income out of it eventually wound up too far apart from EMI's.

Now when we need funding for a large project, we look for a sponsor. A couple weeks ago, my band held an eight-mile musical street parade through Los Angeles, courtesy of Range Rover. They brought no cars, signage or branding; they just asked that we credit them in the documentation of it. A few weeks earlier, we released a music video made in partnership with Samsung, and in February, one was underwritten by State Farm.

We had complete creative control in the productions. At the end of each clip we thanked the company involved, and genuinely, because we truly are thankful. We got the money we needed to make what we want, our fans enjoyed our videos for free, and our corporate Medicis got what their marketing departments were after: millions of eyes and goodwill from our fans. While most bands struggle to wrestle modest video budgets from labels that see videos as loss leaders, ours wind up making us a profit.

We're not the only ones working with brands. Corporate sponsorship of music and musical events in North America will exceed $1 billion in 2010, up from $575 million in 2003, according to William Chipps, author of the IEG Sponsorship Report, a Chicago-based newsletter that tracks and analyzes corporate sponsorship. By comparison, the U.K. music licensing organization PPL reports that record companies' global annual investment in developing and marketing artists stands at $5 billion. The numbers measure slightly different parts of the industry, but from an artist's standpoint, one thing is clear: Outside corporate investment in music is rapidly climbing into the range of the traditional labels'.

Still, this model isn't much use to unknown bands, since companies tend to bet their marketing money on the already established. This brings us to one part of the old record industry that no one seems to know how to replace: the bank. Even in the halcyon days, profitable labels were only successful with about 5% of their artists. Contracts were heavily tilted in favor of labels, so that the huge profits on the few successes paid for the legions of failures. Labels aggregated the music industry's high risks. Even if there are newer, more efficient models for distribution and promotion in the digital era, there aren't many new models for startup investment.

"That's the billion-dollar question," says Ed Donnelly of Aderra Inc., a company that helps touring bands record their live shows and, right there at the venue, sell the recordings to show-goers on custom-decorated USB flash drives (OK Go is a client). "Sure, I work with a lot of young and unheard-of bands," Mr. Donnelly says, "but I'm not a venture capitalist, and I have no interest in trying to totally replace the infrastructure that labels used to provide. I'm trying to give tools to young bands who are doing things their own way. What labels sold were recordings, what we sell is an experience and an emotional connection with the band."

Though his system can't provide the six-figure advances that young bands landed in the 1990s, it can be one crucial puzzle piece in a band's revenue. The unsigned and unmanaged Los Angeles band Killola toured last summer and offered deluxe USB packages that included full albums, live recordings and access to two future private online concerts for $40 per piece. Killola grossed $18,000 and wound up in the black for their tour. Mr. Donnelly says, "I can't imagine they'll be ordering their yacht anytime soon, but traditionally bands at that point in their careers aren't even breaking even on tour."

What Killola is learning is that making a living in music isn't just about selling studio recordings anymore. It's about selling the whole package: themselves. And there are plenty of pioneers leading the way. Top-shelf studio drummer Josh Freese sold his album online with a suite of add-ons. For $250, fans could have lunch with him at P.F. Chang's; he says the 25 slots he offered sold out in a day. One fan sprung for the $20,000 option, which included a miniature golf outing with Mr. Freese and his friends.

Singer Amanda Palmer made over $6,000 in three hours—without leaving her apartment—by personally auctioning off souvenirs from tours and video shoots. The New Orleans trombone rock band Bonerama advertises online that they'll play a show in your home for $10,000.

Not every musician takes the project of selling themselves literally, but the personality and personal lives of musicians are being more openly recognized as valuable assets. The Twitter account of rapper 50 Cent arguably has wider reach than his last album did, and Kanye West has made an art form out of existing in the public eye, holding spontaneous online press conferences and posting rambling blog entries.

This isn't so revolutionary an idea. Pop music has always been a bigger canvas than beats, chords and lyrics alone. In his early days, Elvis's hips were as famous as his voice, and Jimi Hendrix's lighter fluid is as memorable as any of his riffs, but back then the only yardstick to quantify success was the Billboard charts. Now we are untethered from the studio recording as our singular medium, and we measure in Facebook fans, website hits, and— lucky for me—YouTube views.

> "[Bands have] to balance the need to tour set in motion by declining CD sales against the skyrocketing cost of gas, which makes touring more expensive and less profitable."

The Poor Economy and Higher Gas Prices Are Hurting Touring

Luciana Lopez

Luciana Lopez is a staff writer for the Portland, Oregon, newspaper the Oregonian *and a writer for* Juice *and* Urb *magazines. In the following viewpoint, she reports that bands are relying more heavily on touring for income as CD sales fall, but that rising gas prices make touring more and more expensive, while the economic downturn has meant that fewer people are attending concerts. The result, she concludes, is that bands are finding it very difficult to break even.*

As you read, consider the following questions:

1. According to Lopez, how is the band Apollo Sunshine trying to beat high gas prices?

Luciana Lopez, "Band on the Run—From High Gas Prices," *The Oregonian*, June 16, 2008. Republished with permission of publisher, conveyed through Copyright Clearance Center, Inc.

2. How much does the author estimate that it cost Kenny Chesney to make the trip from Portland to Las Vegas?

3. How do concertgoers pay touring costs, according to Lopez?

Tune up the bikes and scrape up the french-fry grease: It's summer touring season for bands. As gas prices climb ever upward, musicians have had to get creative at something more than their music. Portland band Blind Pilot, for example, is traveling under pedal power, and nationally touring psych-rockers Apollo Sunshine are converting their van to run on vegetable oil. There's an easier way to save gas money, though: Portland rocker Michael Dean Damron is just flat-out canceling dates.

Paying for Gas

Different solutions, but all applied to the same problem: how to balance the need to tour set in motion by declining CD sales against the skyrocketing cost of gas, which makes touring more expensive and less profitable.

"It's completely essential to tour," says Kevin O'Connor, half of the electro-acoustic Portland duo Talkdemonic and manager for the Lucky Madison indie record label. An unknown band might get away with skipping a tour to focus on its home base, he says, but for any kind of growth, hitting the road just isn't optional.

The numbers bear that out. Promoting an album can cost an indie label $6,000 or $7,000, O'Connor calculates. If a CD costs $6 or $7 to produce, that's about 1,000 CDs sold just to break even—much less to pay a band. That's why so many bands, especially small indie outfits, have traditionally made their money on the road—perhaps a few hundred dollars a night.

But a $200 door guarantee doesn't stretch nearly as far these days. Talkdemonic, for example, travels in a van that gets close to 17 miles a gallon on the highway "if we don't drive over 70 mph,"

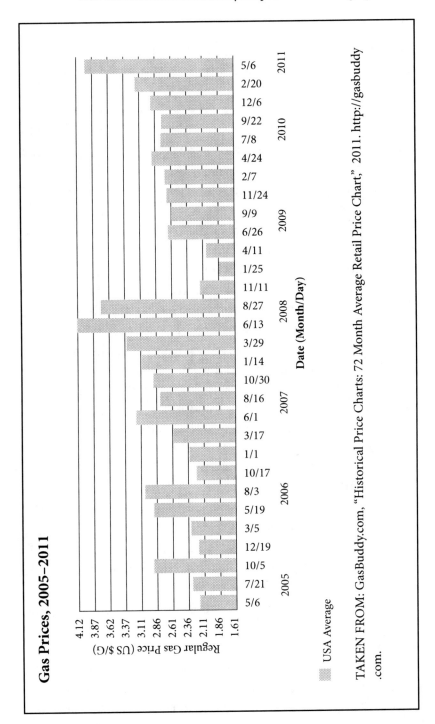

Gas Prices, 2005–2011

TAKEN FROM: GasBuddy.com, "Historical Price Charts: 72 Month Average Retail Price Chart," 2011. http://gasbuddy.com.

O'Connor says. Covering the 635 miles to San Francisco takes about 37 gallons of gas each way. With gas well over $4, that's more than $300 for a round trip. And the problem becomes apparent.

That's especially the case out West, said Damron, where cities big enough to hold shows are spread farther apart. "I just had to cancel shows in Denver," he said. "I can't go as far as Denver. I can go as far as Salt Lake (City)."

Not that big tours necessarily have it much easier. Sure, [country star] Kenny Chesney charged $37.75 to $76 a ticket when he played the Amphitheater at Clark County [near Portland] on June 3, but his traveling expenses reach into the tens of thousands of dollars. On his current tour, Chesney requires 18 trucks and 10 buses, says Steve Hoker, driver coordinator with the Nashville-based Hemphill Brothers Coach Co., whose clients have populated many a Billboard chart. The buses, which weigh about 56,000 pounds fully loaded and have 240-gallon gas tanks, cost about $1 a mile to operate; the 350-gallon trucks are slightly costlier, since they haul more weight (up to 80,000 pounds). A rough estimate reveals that the 1,000-mile trip from Portland to Las Vegas, where Chesney had a June 6 [2008] stop, cost upward of $28,000.

Tour Economics

That would be bad enough, but even as the cost of gas keeps rising, the number of albums sold annually keeps falling. In 2004, Nielsen SoundScan tallied 666.7 million albums (CDs and digital) sold in the United States. By 2007, the number [had] plummeted to 501 million. This year [2010] looks even worse: If album sales continue at the same rate as the first five months of the year, when 171.8 million sold, the final number will be around 412.3 million.

Tour economics aren't for bands alone, either. Concertgoers, ultimately, pay the touring costs, either through higher ticket prices or higher prices for merchandise such as T-shirts and posters. At Jimmy Mak's, the Portland jazz club recently called a "dream venue" by *Esquire* magazine, bands have asked for higher guarantees in the past month or two, notes club owner Jim Makarounis. But giving bands a bigger check upfront doesn't mean they'll generate more ticket sales.

"We are a business driven just 100 percent on discretionary income," Makarounis explains. So with a tighter economy squeezing music consumers, raising door prices might not be an option. Raising a band's guarantee "does throw a little more risk into the equation."

Higher gas prices won't affect the touring plans of one Portland band, though. Blind Pilot's members are setting out by bike this year to promote their new album, out June 21, says drummer Ryan Dobrowski. Gas prices weren't the sole motivator—they've traveled by bike before—but the bikes make the tour much more affordable than if they had to pay hundreds of dollars for gas. On their previous bike tour, Dobrowski said, "we were kind of flying by the seat of our pants. We were definitely making enough money to just keep going forward."

Dobrowski has designed a drum set that fits inside itself for easy biking, and the bass player is building a trailer case for his upright bass. The band plans to update its West Coast itinerary online so fans can follow the cycling route.

Still, even a bike tour has its costs, Dobrowski noted.

"It might not be all that financially better," he said. "You do want to eat all the time."

| "There are plenty of ways to generate income besides selling records, if you are willing to think ahead of the curve."

Independent Artists Need to Explore New Marketing and Revenue Options

Jeff McQuilkin

Jeff McQuilkin is a musician, songwriter, and blogger at The Developing Artist. In the following viewpoint he argues that as recording sales collapse, indie musicians need to find new ways to make music pay. He suggests live performances, selling merchandise, and giving away music as free samples tied to for-sale products with extra bonuses. He also suggests selling music through a subscription service and getting music on streaming radio channels.

As you read, consider the following questions:

1. What merchandise does McQuilkin suggest that bands could sell at concerts?

2. What does the author say that Sam Phillips has done to make money from her music?

3. What is Pandora, and how might it help independent musicians generate income, according to McQuilkin?

If you don't already know that the music industry is in a time of upheaval, you either have your head in the sand or are not a musician (which is okay by the way—I mean, it's okay not to be a musician, it's not okay to have your head in the sand . . . oh, heck, nevermind).

Alternative Strategies

Anyway, the changes going on in music deeply affect how musicians (especially indie musicians) make money. While social networking now helps independent bands to reach fans more directly, digital downloading has made it easier than ever for fans to get music without paying for it, and attempts to enforce paid downloads have been largely unfruitful. It remains to be seen how all this turmoil will work out, but if you are a forward-thinking type of individual, you'll see the wisdom in coming up with alternative money-making ideas rather than relying on music sales as your primary income source. Chances are, if you're an indie musician reading this, you've already thought about (or tried) some of the ideas I've put down here. But read on—maybe you'll find something you hadn't thought about yet.

It used to be that live performances/touring was a way to sell more records. Nowadays, especially with indie musicians, the live performance and the record seem to be reversing roles: now the live performance is the main event, and the record is the advertisement. It helps to have a record to sell at your shows, but bands that are out gigging regularly have a better shot at regular income, with or without a record. More bands are focusing less on being "studio bands" and more on "playing out." As one veteran musician friend of mine put it, "If you're willing to play live, you'll always have a job in music."

Merchandising is rapidly becoming a major income stream for smaller bands. As a band or artist, you are actually developing your own "brand", and merchandise with your name on it is a way of keeping your brand in front of the public. When fans come to your shows, it is a great idea to have band t-shirts, hats, stickers and other merch[andise] available for them to buy, along with your records if you have them. Sometimes merchandise sales generate even more money than the show itself. You can even sell your merchandise on the Internet, if you have a website.

Now, I can hear some of you saying (PG Version), *"Now, wait just a cotton-pickin' minute. How is giving away my music an alternative money-making idea?"* Well, actually it comes from an old marketing technique: Give something to the customers for free, and they'll *buy* something else from you. In this case, the music itself becomes the freebie, usually as a free digital download. You can give away a song or two, or a full album. Where you make the money is by offering an *additional* special product that can't be downloaded, like a "special edition" CD with extra features and merchandise attached. You might be surprised how many fans will pay to receive something "special" in addition to their free download.

In line with this, another thing lots of bands are doing these days is making their albums available for download and letting people pay what they decide—kind of an "honor system." Yes, people will still take it without paying for it, but they'll probably feel bad for doing it. And that's what you want to do—make people feel bad. (Not really.) Seriously, you might be surprised at how many of your fans will actually pay for your record when you give them this option.

Thinking Ahead of the Curve

Veteran recording artist Sam Phillips (www.samphillips.com) recently offered a special subscription to her fans. For a one-time fee, she offered fans year-long access to exclusive music as she produced it (equal to 5 EPs and one full-length), documentary videos, written notes and more—literally allowing fans "front-row" access to her creative process through the year. You can put your own spin on this idea, but subscriptions like this are potentially a great way not only to make some money, but also to build loyalty with your fans. . . .

SoundExchange monitors the music played on all cable, Internet and satellite radio outlets, and pays royalties to the musicians who made the music. If you can get your music up on Pandora, Sirius or XM [all streaming radio channels], and other places like that, it can be a great way to get exposure, and make some passive income.

Now, don't get me wrong; you should keep making recordings and trying to sell them. You deserve to be paid for your art, in any way possible. But in this time of change in the music business, finding alternative ways to make money for your band is never a bad idea. There are plenty of ways to generate income besides selling records, if you are willing to think ahead of the curve.

> "With a little thought and organization,
> you can use [social networking]
> websites to great effect with very little
> time investment."

Musicians Need Not Spend Too Much Time on Online Marketing

Cameron Mizell

Cameron Mizell is a musician and the founder of the website Musician Wages. In the following viewpoint he argues that musicians need to create an online presence, but they should spend as little time doing so as they can. He argues that the first thing musicians need to do is create great music. Great music, he says, will encourage fans to create online content about the band. Beyond that, he says, musicians should focus carefully on the online networking sites that will be most useful for them, and should find timesaving ways to use those sites.

As you read, consider the following questions:

1. According to Mizell, what should be an indie musician's focus and why?

2. If you're a musician, what does the author say you should do the next time somebody tells you you should be doing something that has nothing to do with creating music?

3. Why does Mizell see it as a victory when he discovers that a particular online publicity effort is a failure?

For the independent, D.I.Y. [do-it-yourself] musician, establishing a balance between online and offline efforts is becoming increasingly difficult. It seems that every new social networking site that pops up is one more task to add to your overflowing list of things to do. With each website you're trying to fill the shoes of musician, marketer, sales person and booking agent if not more. It's a full time job in and of itself—simply too much for musicians who also hold down some sort of job outside of music to help support themselves. How is one supposed to keep up?

This article is not about how to keep up, rather it's about how to ignore the noise. To be blunt, there are people out there trying to make money from you. This is a classic case of products and services that we didn't know we needed until they existed. In most cases, we don't need them. If they're not trying to sell you something, they're just trying to get your attention or your internet traffic. I'm not blaming these people; they only exist because independent musicians make a good market. We have only ourselves to blame for all these distractions.

It is entirely possible to ignore most of what's happening online and still have a large internet presence. The beauty of the internet is that your presence can exist without [your] sitting in front of a computer. Here's what I suggest.

First, Create Great Content

Great music should make up the bulk of your great content. Without a doubt, this is the hardest part, and it should be. Our specialty is music, and we should be better at making music than everybody else. The better you are, the less of the other stuff you'll have to do. More people will do that work for you; your fans will do that work for you.

For example, I have a few friends that recently started a band in New York City. They have MySpace and Facebook pages for the band as well as individual pages, but that's it. Nothing special, and far less than what a new-media/social networking guru would advise. If judged by their internet presence alone, ignoring their actual content, you'd probably blow them off.

They spend all their time practicing, and several days a week they set up to busk in the subway or Central Park. They burn CDs to sell for $5 and have cards available with their band name and MySpace URL. They also have a notebook for collecting email addresses.

They're making good money in tips and selling the CDs, but what's amazing is how many people are taking notice. Simply because they are so *good*, people stop, listen, and take note of who they are. There are several videos of them on YouTube created by commuters. We've found a few blogs where the authors just wanted to share the experience of listening to the band in the middle of their hectic day.

The best content is not even created by the band, it's created by fans—people who invested their own time for the sake of spreading the word about some great music. That sounds pretty old school, doesn't it?

The rest of your content should be *about* music (but not necessarily yours) without talking directly about *the* music. The best approach is to simply be yourself and write about how music is a big part of your life. For example, if you're training for a marathon, blog about your morning run and share your playlist, perhaps as an iMix. You can even sidetrack to discuss your hobbies or your favorite TV shows, things non-musicians can relate to. As long as there's a link to your website or album somewhere on the web page, you don't need to remind everyone that you're a musician all the time.

Have a Purpose in All You Do

If you want to waste your time, [then just] don't have a clue what you're trying to do. To avoid wasting time, get focused, be honest with yourself and hold others accountable to be honest with you. The next time somebody tells you that you should be doing something that has nothing to do with writing or playing music, ask questions. Find out the real reason why they think you should create another online profile for your band or read a book about the music business.

Perhaps one of the best things you can do for your music is create a blog to hold yourself accountable. Turn it into a journal about something you're working on musically. You could blog about making an album, or touring, or just write about what you're practicing. I find that writing about things I'm planning on doing makes me do it sooner than later because I'm sorting it out in my head so the *doing* part is easier. Simply the act of writing this article is helping me figure out ways to be more efficient with my time online. And we've all heard about the stunts that involve writing and posting a recording of a new song every day for a month, or something similar. Sure, those are publicity stunts, but they're also exercises in creativity. Difficult exercises. . . .

Go to Your Audience

Back to the example of my friends' band—they've found the places in the subway or Central Park that make them the most money. They've found they do best playing for the locals, not tourists. Just because there are more people that want to spend their money in Times Square it doesn't mean that's the best location for them to play their music.

Similarly, each website or social network draws different crowds, and the goal is to find the one or two places where your music appeals to the site's existing audience. It's better to find ten people that really like what you're doing and want to spread the word rather than shouting at 10,000 people that are all ignoring you. Besides, if those ten people can share your content with their friends, via Facebook, Twitter, Tumblr, etc., your audience will multiply.

Also, consider the type of connections you need to make. For my type of musician (one with original content), Facebook hasn't been very effective, but Twitter is. For a musician like Dave Hahn (a contract musician), Facebook is the better networking tool. Figure out where like-minded musicians have the most success and focus on that website.

Schedule and Feed Your Blogs

There are certain times during the week internet traffic is high and people are more likely to respond to your content. Posting content, or links to your content, during these times is a great way to increase traffic to your website and ultimately get more people to listen to your music. This also allows you to spread out one day's work over the course of a week or more. Some days I get two or more ideas for blog posts, so I tackle them while they're fresh in my mind but schedule them a week apart.

I also schedule most of my Twitter updates on Sundays using HootSuite. Many of these tweets are links to content I find interesting, but I'll also work in some of the "this is what I'm doing" updates. I can do that simply because I plan out my week on Sundays. I'll go ahead and schedule a tweet for Thursday about the rehearsal I have that day so I don't have to worry about it later. A few times throughout each day I'll log into Twitter using TweetDeck and respond to people's replies and see what's going on, but I'm never logged in for more than a few minutes. There are many blog posts out there about how to use Twitter effectively, so that's not what I'm trying to discuss here. Rather, I want to make the point that with a little thought and organization, you can use these kinds of websites to great effect with very little time investment.

Along with scheduling posts, most websites today can aggregate content from other sites. This is a great way to stake out more internet territory without adding extra work. This can usually be done using RSS feeds, and with a little formatting you can make it look pretty slick. Along with writing for Musician Wages, I have a personal blog over at Blogger which feeds into my Tumblr page. I also can easily create links on Tumblr and Facebook to the articles and blog posts I write. It makes my life easy, and it sends my content to a larger audience.

There are some websites and widgets out there that can update multiple social networking sites at once, but I've never used them. Instead, all the important information that changes regularly, like my gig calendar, is easily found on the homepage of my website. I prefer to keep things simple and just include a link to my site from all my various profiles.

Use Metadata and Keywords

This should be a no-brainer, but it's amazing how many musicians I see not making the most out of their content with at least minimally optimized keywords [that is, words that tell a search engine specifically what a post is about.]. At first, you're going to have to generate your own traffic, but after a while search engines can do a lot of the work for you. However, they won't do you any good if your blog posts are full of typos or you just fail to mention in words what is happening on this web page. Search engines look at the text that's viewable by visitors, so don't be afraid to brand each page with your full name or your band's name. If you're out in the world doing your thing and getting people to remember your name, make sure they can find you when they type it into Google.

Unfortunately, the only way to know whether or not something will work for you is to try it out. That takes time, and your time is valuable and better spent working on your music. However, when something comes along that you think might work out for you, consider allowing yourself anywhere from one week to two months to try it out. If you've never started a blog, dedicate one night a week to write something for a couple months. This might take a couple hours of work a week, but that's not a terrible amount of time. And you'll know whether or not it's right for you by the end of two months.

I've gotten to the point where I dedicate about two hours a week to trying something new online. I don't view the failures as a waste of time. In fact, I consider it a victory when an idea never gains traction—that's one less task to worry about. I've accepted routine failures as part of the route to genuine long-term success.

Keep in mind, this is a long-term undertaking. There's no secret to creating a strong online presence overnight no matter how much time you spend on it in one sitting. Build gradually and purposefully upon your previous content, and make sure it's all riding on the shoulders of great music.

Periodical and Internet Sources Bibliography

The following articles have been selected to supplement the diverse views presented in this chapter.

Jeff Balke	"Touring Can't Replace CD Sales," *Houston Chronicle Broken Record* blog, June 18, 2008. http://blogs.chron.com.
Economist	"What's Working in Music: Having a Ball," October 7, 2010.
Lisa Respers France	"Is the Death of the CD Looming?," CNN.com, July 20, 2010. www.cnn.com.
Bob Gentry	"A Well-Oiled Indie Music Website," *Bob Gentry Journal*, April 21, 2011. www.bobgentry.com.
Mike Melanson	"Report: Digital Music Sales Will Surpass CDs in 2012," Read Write Web, January 14, 2010. www.readwriteweb.com.
Dave Parrack	"Music Sales Chart Reveals the Truth—CD Bubble Was Never Going to Be Sustained," Tech.Blorge, February 17, 2011. http://tech.blorge.com.
Glenn Peoples	"Analysis: Lower CD Prices Could Provide a Shot in the Arm," *Billboard*, March 24, 2010.
Matthew Perpetua	"Vinyl Sales Increase Despite Industry Slump," *Rolling Stone*, January 6, 2011.
Erick Schonfeld	"Ian Rogers on the Death of the Music CD Business: 'I Don't Care,'" TechCrunch, November 19, 2008. http://techcrunch.com.
Mark Sweney	"Global Recorded Music Sales Fall Almost $1.5bn amid Increased Piracy," *Guardian* (Manchester, UK), March 28, 2011.

OPPOSING
VIEWPOINTS®
SERIES

CHAPTER 3

What Role Do Record Labels Play in the Twenty-First Century?

Chapter Preface

Major labels are large, international record companies. According to the article "Record Companies and Labels" on Bemuso.com, major labels control around 70 percent of music sales worldwide.

Given this huge market share, it is surprising how few major labels there are. Through the 1990s, there were six major labels—Warner Music Group, EMI, Sony Music, BMG Music, Universal Music Group, and Polygram. In 1998, Polygram was absorbed by Universal, leaving only five. In 2004, Sony and BMG joined into Sony BMG, five years later morphing into Sony Music Entertainment. Today there are, therefore, only four major labels.

Universal Music Group, or UMG, is owned by French conglomerate Vivendi and is the label "with the highest record sales," according to Linda Laban in a October 14, 2009, article on the website Spinner. Like all the majors, UMG has a number of subsidiary or sublabels. For UMG the most important of these are Geffen, Interscope, Island, and Motown. Among Universal's most important artists are U2, 50 Cent, the Black Eyed Peas, Kanye West, and Mariah Carey.

Sony Music Entertainment is the second largest major label. It is owned by the Japanese company Sony through the Sony Corporation of America. It's important subsidiary labels include Columbia/Epic Label Group, RCA/Jive Label Group, Sony Music Nashville, and Legacy Recordings. Major Sony artists include Beyoncé, Britney Spears, Shakira, and AC/DC.

The EMI Group is the third largest major label. It is historically British, and is best known for being the label of the Beatles. Its subsidiary labels include Capitol, EMI, Mute, and Virgin. Besides the Beatles, other important artists on EMI include the Rolling Stones, Kylie Minogue, and Coldplay.

The Warner Music Group is the smallest of the major labels in terms of sales. It started as "an offshoot to Warner Bros. movie studio, releasing movie soundtracks," according to Linda Laban. Its major subsidiary labels include Atlantic, Asylum, Lava, Reprise, and Rhino. Major artists include Green Day, Madonna, and Alanis Morissette.

Despite their size and influence, the Big Four have been struggling as the music industry has transformed in recent years. EMI in particular has had serious financial troubles. In February 2011 it was seized by the American bank Citigroup after it was unable to pay its debts. The bank plans to sell the company, and there is a chance that "the once greatest of our music companies might cease to exist altogether," according to Brian Southall in a March 2, 2011, article in London's *Daily Mirror*. Thus, it seems possible that in the near future there may be only the Big Three major labels—and perhaps, down the road, even fewer than that.

The following viewpoints examine the ongoing role of labels, both major and independent, in the changing music industry.

> *"Labels are transforming themselves to help musicians in the digital age."*

Major Labels Must Change to Stay Viable

Adam Frucci

Adam Frucci is a a senior editor at the website DVICE, and a former associate editor at Gizmodo. In the following viewpoint he contends that record labels are struggling to remain relevant. Album sales are dropping, he notes, physical stores are less and less important, and bands can often promote themselves effectively through the Internet. Many services that labels used to provide, he argues, are no longer important. However, he maintains that labels still provide useful contacts and the ability to handle business details for artists. Record labels probably will not disappear, he concludes, but they need to change radically.

As you read, consider the following questions:

1. According to Frucci, how much does it cost to get an album up on major digital stores?
2. What is a 360 deal, as described by the author?
3. *Billboard's* Glenn Peoples says what kind of bands need radio and brick-and-mortar retail?

It's lousy to be a record label. Profits are tanking, bands are angry—OK Go just ditched [major label] EMI—and YouTube and BitTorrent changed the game. Still, some labels are transforming themselves to help musicians in the digital age.

"Change or Die"

"Change or Die" may sound like hyperbole, or an idle threat, but for the music business, the two alternatives have never been more real. EMI may very well go extinct *in the coming months*, and all of the major labels are fighting losing battles. But all is not lost.

The traditional role of a record label, in the broadest sense, is to bankroll a band until they start making lots of money, at which point the label gets to keep most of it. They own the master recordings a band makes, and by taking on this ownership they put all of their resources behind selling said recordings.

This setup makes sense when bands lacked the wherewithal to produce and record their own albums and when manufacturing and distributing physical copies of albums and marketing said albums costs hundreds of thousands of dollars. It also makes sense when a popular album will sell millions of copies at $15 a pop.

But that's definitely not the case now. Record stores are dying at an alarming rate, and fewer and fewer people are buying CDs every day. It's safe to say that the current generation of teenagers has never perused record stores as a normal activity; it's all downhill from here for physical music sales. And FM radio isn't doing too hot either. In short, everything that the music industry has known to be true for the last few decades is quickly turning to dust. Big labels can still bank on country, R&B and pop acts, but the bottom has already fallen out on alternative groups and other internet-friendly genres. And that's just the beginning.

The Old, Dead Way of Doing Business

The way bands operate has changed so much in the last decade that what a label can provide and what bands require of a label has changed drastically, faster than labels have been able to adapt.

Manufacturing and distribution used to be the cornerstone of a label's business; every major label owned its own plants to make the albums and also dealt with shipping the albums worldwide. Today, only Sony still owns plants that manufacture CDs, with the other three big labels outsourcing manufacturing to them. But they all still have reps who have to go out to record stores and make sure that their albums are getting proper shelf space. They have to deal with defects and returns. There are lots of resources required to deal with the manufacture and distribution of a physical product, but that physical product is quickly headed towards irrelevancy.

The biggest music stores are now virtual, so there's no need for someone to go gladhand every Sam Goody [music store] manager so they give you endcap space for *Use Your Illusion II* [a 1991 album by Guns 'n' Roses]. The iTunes Music Store [a digital music store] sells 25% of the music sold in America as of last August [2009] and that number is definitely going up, not down.

According to the IFPI [International Federation of the Phonographic Industry], physical sales of music dropped 15.4% globally between 2007 and 2008. But in that same year, digital sales rose 24.1%. And Nielsen SoundScan numbers show that the number of units sold between 2006 and 2009 rose from 1 billion per year to 1.7 billion per year, with a unit referring to either an album or a song sold. It's a significant increase, but when someone buying three songs counts the same as someone buying three CDs, you can see why the labels are losing money despite the positive-sounding stat.

But for unsigned bands, companies such as TuneCore and CD Baby act as middlemen between them and digital storefronts like iTunes for very small amounts of money; getting your album up on major stores such as iTunes, Amazon and eMusic will set you back about $47 through TuneCore. And you retain all ownership of your music and keep all royalties, unlike working with a record label.

And TuneCore's internal numbers show that online sales are growing even faster for independent acts than those already well established. TuneCore CEO Jeff Price told me that between 2007 and 2009, TuneCore artists have gone from earning $7–8 million a year to $31 million, with $60 million in earnings projected for 2010. That's insane growth, to be sure, but it's got a long way to go before it represents a sizable proportion of global music sales. To put things in perspective, the IFPI recorded $4.9 billion in sales for 2008.

Furthermore, these days it's easier than ever for musicians to record music without an expensive studio. Software such as Reason, Pro Tools and Logic can be bought for $300 or less, and run on a mid-range laptop. Cheap mics and gear can be found all over eBay and Craigslist. Tie everything together with a $200 to $500 mic preamp analog-to-digital/digital-to-analog box, and you have a mini-studio in your bedroom.

And music blogs have turned the way artists are discovered on its head. It used to be that high-paid A&R [artists and repertoire] executives would scour clubs to find underground bands to sign, acting as the filter between the millions of mediocre bands and the discriminating public. Today, obsessive music fans scour clubs and the web for free, discovering new acts and writing about them on blogs. Labels then discover bands from these blogs. The A&R system is no longer as relevant.

Marketing and promotion, another cornerstone service that labels provide, has also been transformed by the web. You no longer need radio play and ads in *Rolling Stone* to get your band noticed. When a band makes a music video, there's less of a need for a major label with contacts at MTV to push it through official channels to get it noticed. These days, you can just throw it up on YouTube and get it noticed by some music—or gadget—blogs. The fact that it's a simple click or two from video appreciation to buying actual music is worth more than any paper ad in any dying magazine.

The Rise and Fall of EMI

There is no question that EMI is right up there in the pantheon of great British companies—it signed The Beatles, owned the HMV Dog & Trumpet trademark, opened and ran the world-famous Abbey Road Studios, sacked The Sex Pistols, and re-leased records by [English pop star] Cliff Richard for 30 years while also developing high-profile defense, medical, leisure, and film divisions.

In fact there was a time when you could walk down London's Oxford Street and give your hard-earned cash to EMI at every turn. You could stay in a hotel, visit a coffee bar, buy an album in a record shop, lunch in a restaurant, see a movie in a cinema and finally dance the night away in a disco—and EMI would own it all. . . .

EMI owned or was involved in all these things, but it was its music business that caught the imagination and interest of millions of record buyers the world over; its roster in-cluded many of the world's leading recording artists assigned to world-famous labels ranging from HMV to Parlophone, Capitol to Columbia and Angel to Harvest. . . .

But in recent years . . . the company has suffered a steep decline.

Brian Southall, The Rise and Fall of EMI
Records, *2009.*

As Voyno from the musicians-as-entrepreneurs blog New Rockstar Philosophy told me, it's very possible for a band to use the internet to replace much of what a label provides:

There are artists on YouTube who use creative on-the-cheap strategies to garner millions of views that direct traffic to their main site, iTunes pages, Facebook page and bandcamp.com profile. They then build an e-mail/text subscription from their new fans, which allows them to offer new merchandise, tickets for shows and other related info directly to fans. The web traffic analytics from all their sites can help them plan successful tours, target Facebook ads, and make better decisions on how to move forward.

These changes have shaken the foundation of the industry, and the biggest labels have borne the brunt of the losses that these changes wrought.

Tough Times for Major Labels

EMI is *bleeding* money. Earlier this month [March 2010], it reported a whopping $2.4 *billion* loss, which, when added to its prior debts, puts it $4.5 billion in debt to CitiGroup. It owes Citi $160 million this month, and it's facing a restructuring plan that'll require an additional investment from its parent company.

EMI is owned by Terra Firma Capital Partners, a British private equity firm that also owns waste management companies, gas stations, residential home builders and movie theaters. To them, the art EMI is releasing is about as important as the trash that Waste Recycling Group collects. If it doesn't make them money, it isn't worth keeping around, 80 years of history or not.

Billboard's Senior Editorial Analyst Glenn Peoples told me that it's not for lack of trying that EMI finds itself in this position. "Labels have cut as many costs as they possibly can, they've taken fewer risks, they've signed fewer artists and tried to make safer bets," he says.

"They're doing what they can, but the revenue might not be there to support the way they do business. So it's very possible that the recorded music division of EMI will be sold off and will go elsewhere. An acquisition by Warner Music Group is a possibility, and that would take it down to three majors in recorded music, and that'd be pretty drastic and a lot of concentration between three companies."

An EMI Music spokesperson told me, "EMI Music is doing well. We've reported revenue growth, despite a declining market, and strong operating profit and margin improvement, both in the last financial year and in the current year." But if they can't convince Terra Firma that they have a way out of the quagmire they're in, the possibility of the number of major labels to dropping to three is very real.

And if that happens, what of those remaining three? Universal Music Group is owned by French media conglomerate Vivendi, a company with stakes in the Universal and Canal movie studios and the video game publisher Activision Blizzard amongst other holdings. Sony Music Entertainment is obviously a division of Sony, and we all know Sony has had problems of its own lately. Warner Music Group is the only major without a parent company to answer to, as it spun off from Time Warner in 2004, and its revenue dropped about $3.5 billion last year.

All Is Not Lost

But all is not lost, and the death of the record label as a business is not a foregone conclusion. Labels from EMI down to the smallest indie labels are racing to change the way they do business. And they still have quite a bit to offer.

Ra Ra Riot is a band from Syracuse, NY, who's currently prepping their second album from indie label Barsuk Records. Barsuk is a true indie based out of Seattle, featuring bands such as Death Cab for Cutie, Mates of State, Nada Surf and They Might Be Giants in addition to Ra Ra Riot.

I talked to Josh Roth, Ra Ra Riot's manager, about the reasons bands still have for signing with a label. One big positive that signing to a label provides a band, he told me, is giving them legitimacy. "I think right now with the internet, there are just so many bands out there that it's easy to go unnoticed," he told me. "There still is a certain charm to having a label saying 'We like this band and we're going to sign them and you should take a listen.' With the amount of bands that are out there, it's hard to filter what is actually good now."

Furthermore, as outlets such as radio and MTV have become less relevant, new venues for being heard and getting paid have opened up. "Commercials are becoming much more relevant," Ra Ra Riot guitarist Milo Bonacci told me.

"That's how a lot of bands get paid or get their music out there. That's how a lot of people hear a song for the first time. I feel like commercials are taking the place of commercial radio." And to get on a commercial, it sure helps to be signed to a label with a nice licensing department.

Of course, there are different types of record labels. A major label, such as EMI, has a lot more money to throw around and can make more promises, but contracts with majors can end up with artists further in the hole due to these deep pockets. As Bonacci told me, "There's more risk. There's more fuel to propel you forward up front, but that's no guarantee." That same fuel could blow up in your face. We've seen how bands who don't hit it big can end up "owing" their major label hundreds of thousands of dollars, after all.

Indie labels (true indie labels, not boutiques under the umbrella of a major) have less resources and therefore will give bands less to recoup. Indies also will often offer the artist a chance to interact with top brass, something that is almost never done at a major. Indies are presumably owned by passionate music fans rather than gigantic multinational holding companies, which is important when a band needs to know that a label is 100% behind them, according to RRR's Bonacci.

And signing to an indie instantly connects you to that label's fans, Bonacci says. "Nobody really cares about Sony records or Universal. You don't seek out stuff that's being released on Universal as a fan. Independent labels, be it Domino or SubPop or whatever, *those* labels have fans."

Indie labels seem to have a better chance of adapting and surviving in tumultuous times. Since for the most part they're private companies with few employees, they're able to make drastic changes in their business models much more quickly than major labels. But that doesn't mean they'll all survive; famed indie label Touch and Go closed down last year, and in addition to repping bands such as TV on the Radio, Ted Leo and the Pharmacists, !!! and Blonde Redhead, they also handled distribution for other venerable indies such as Drag City, Kill Rock Stars, Jade Tree and Merge. It was a huge blow to the indie label scene.

Getting a Cut of Everything

The way labels are moving to stay alive is by becoming involved in the places that bands still make money, such as touring and merchandising. Traditionally, labels only made money off records sold, while any profits made from t-shirts or posters sold on the road went to the band. After all, if the label just owns the master recordings, it can only make money off the sale of said recordings, not any ancillary profits that come from things like touring.

But now some labels are pushing what are called 360 deals, which involve them in virtually everything an artist does. One of the most famous 360 deals was EMI's 2002 deal with Robbie Williams, which was worth a whopping £80 million, giving EMI a piece of basically everything that Williams touched. That didn't go so well, with Williams threatening to withhold albums from the label and trying to get out of his contract. But last week [in March 2010], according to UK trade paper *Music Week*, Williams' manager Tim Clark publicly came out in support of the embattled label, saying, "My own view is Citigroup would be mad at this stage not to keep EMI on as a going concern. It just would be bonkers."

In any case, 360 deals and general diversification are what big labels such as EMI are looking to move into, according to *Billboard*'s Glenn Peoples. "They're definitely diversifying and they're actually getting into agencies, artist management, concert promotion. There's really no area that the four majors are not pursuing right now."

These deals make the most sense for huge acts with lots of opportunities for branding and licensing. . . . [Two examples are rapper and producer] Dr. Dre's Beats headphones and Lady Gaga's new Creative Director "job" at Polaroid. Both those acts are signed to Interscope, a sub-label of Universal that's clearly pushing artists towards these new revenue streams. But many smaller acts are still reluctant to give a label a slice of the entire pie with such a wide-reaching deal.

The fact of the matter is that bands do still need someone working for them, 360 deal or not. For some bands, just having a small team of a dedicated manager, publicist and lawyer who can handle the nitty-gritty of online sales, tour organization, merchandising and marketing will be enough for them. But many can still benefit from the huge networks that labels have with their contacts in every facet of the industry. Sure, you can print your own t-shirts, but a label with contacts with clothing manufacturers, stores and distributors can make that process a lot easier. And just how much of this work do you want to do yourself?

360 deals don't make sense for all bands; Ra Ra Riot manager Roth isn't sold on them. "A lot of labels are also now branching into management because the manager is involved with everything going on with a band. Labels will try to be like a full-service company to a band, but I don't think it'll be very popular." He worries that bands will be setting themselves up to be taken advantage of even more by labels if they give up merchandising and touring profits to them. Having an independent team working for a band and playing middleman between them and the label makes sure there's someone deeply involved in "business stuff" that still has their best interests at heart.

And it makes sense that a manager would be wary of labels moving into their territory, but there's still a distinction between label and manager with these deals. "For example, a new artist signed to a multi-rights deal may use the major label's merchandise company and e-commerce division in addition to its publishing and recorded music companies," Peoples says. "In the past, a manager could pick and choose which merch, e-commerce, publishing and record companies it wanted to work with. Now they're more likely to be under the same umbrella."

Bigger Changes

Sometimes, a band's management team can replace what a label does entirely. Just yesterday, OK Go announced it was splitting with EMI, whom they didn't have the greatest relationship with, to strike out on their own with a new company called Paracadute. Paracadute is basically OK Go's own team to handle management, promotion and distribution of their records. "The things that a major has to offer above and beyond anybody else are the things that OK Go really didn't need so much," Peoples says. "And that's radio promotion and access to brick and mortar retail. If you're going to create nearly all of your consumer awareness through cheaply made YouTube videos, you don't need this big promotional and distribution system behind you."

But not all bands can do what OK Go has done. The digital world looks a lot more accessible when only viewed through the lens of rock acts. "If you're an R&B act, if you're a straight up pop act, a country act, you're going to need radio and you're going to need brick and mortar retail, and that's not going to change anytime soon. Things are changing definitely for alternative rock, rock and indie, but some genres sell a lot better in digital than other genres."

But clearly, the money that's to be made in music is no longer just in album sales. And bands seem to be presented with a choice: they can either allow labels to become more involved in everything that they do, and give up money that used to go exclusively to them in the process, or strike out on their own. Either way, they'll entering a landscape where getting their song on [the television show] Gossip Girl for 40 seconds is more important than any amount of FM radio play, where getting a music video posted to Stereogum is more important than getting it on MTV and where you make more money touring behind an album than selling that same album.

And in order to prove to artists that signing with a label is a better idea than going out on your own, they'll need to make big changes; bigger than they've made so far. "It might be how an addict ends up turning his life around," Peoples says. "He's gotta hit rock bottom. And I dunno if the record industry has hit rock bottom yet, but maybe that's what'll need to happen for there to be really big change."

But at the end of the day, the saving grace of record labels might be a lot more basic than who gets what percentage of merchandise or who deals with distribution. The big question is this: do bands really want to try to make it completely on their own? As Bonacci says, "I don't necessarily want to have all that nitty-gritty stuff to worry about. I'd rather just worry about making music. I don't want to worry about numbers or distribution or marketing or publicity or anything like that. That sounds like a desk job. I used to have a desk job, that's why I'm playing music. Now look at me. I sleep on couches."

> *"Most successful artists on Indie labels*
> *are on imprints of major record labels.*
> *It's the majors providing the manpower,*
> *money and expertise."*

Major Labels Can Do More for Artists Than Indie Labels Can

Brent DeFore

Brent DeFore is the pseudonym of an indie musician. In the following viewpoint, he argues that the major labels are not responsible for the meltdown of the record industry. Instead, he says, the problem is illegal downloading. He further argues that signing with a major label is the only way to make serious money as a musician. He concludes that indie labels and independent artists do not have the time, resources, or expertise to compete with major labels.

As you read, consider the following questions:

1. Why does DeFore say that your chances of getting the big house, the fancy cars, and the private jets are practically zero if you are signed to an indie label?

2. According to the author, why are major labels responsible for even most successful indie label artists?

3. How many CDs are sold by most bands who press a thousand CDs, according to DeFore?

"I don't want to sign with a major record label," seems to come from the lips of *most* songwriters and artists these days. Everybody wants to sign with an Indie label or take the Do-It-Yourself route.

Bigger Staff, Bigger Budget

But there's a problem. Most musicians think that they'll get special treatment being signed to an Indie label because of the small roster. While that's often true, there's another side to signing with an Indie that most bands and artists rarely consider.

Not only are the rosters much smaller, so are the label's staff and budget! Quickly, how many platinum-selling artists [that is, artists with one million album sales] can you think of that are on an Indie label? One, two . . . a few at most? And over what period of time? Years?

TAXI.com president Michael Laskow is outspoken about why a major record label might still be your best bet—at least for the time being. He raised this point while moderating the Major Label A&R [artists and repertoire] panel at last year's TAXI Road Rally, and not one of the thousand musicians in the audience could argue his point. No hands were raised when Laskow asked if anybody in the ballroom had made more than chump change as an independent artist using the Internet as their primary marketing channel.

Yes, the record industry is melting down! But it's not because the major labels can't break an artist. The reason is that 95% of all music consumed in the U.S. is illegally downloaded. If people could steal meat through a wire with relative impunity, wouldn't they?

Would we blame the butchers and grocery stores for a rapid decline in *their* industry?

So, *why* then do we equate the downward spiral of the record industry with major labels ripping off musicians? Yes, they've been heavy handed. Yes, they are about making a profit!

Aren't you?

Don't you want to make money with your music? Lots of money?

Guess what? Your chances of getting the big house, the fancy cars and flying around on private jets are practically zip if you're on an Indie label. Most independent labels only print up 2–3,000 copies of each new release. They have tiny marketing budgets. They can't get you on the big, major market radio stations you need to get played on to have a hit. Every now and then, an indie will have real success, but take a look at the fine print.

Indies Cannot Compete with Majors

Most successful artists on Indie labels are on *imprints* of major record labels. It's the majors providing the manpower, money and expertise to break the artist. But don't be fooled. Most Indies *don't* have major label distribution.

So, if an Indie label only prints a couple thousand units and doesn't have much in the way of cash, tour support, staff or marketing expertise, aren't you better off manufacturing a couple thousand CDs on your own and marketing them through [online music distributors] CD Baby or Tunecore?

Sure, if you don't have a job or a mortgage payment! Can you really spend eighteen hours a day working on being your own label? Do you have tens of thousands of dollars to throw at your marketing? A major label will spend hundreds of thousands or more!

How do you plan on getting your music on the radio? Can you afford to hire a radio promoter? How then, will you compete with the major labels that can and *do*?

Can you afford to drop everything and spend your last dime on touring for a year? A real record label would give you a touring budget—maybe a hundred grand or two for the first year.

Can you match that? You'll need to if you want compete at that level.

Let me put it to you this way: How many web sites do you currently have your music on? MySpace, ReverbNation, Facebook, Twitter, iTunes? Uh-huh.

And how much money have you made as a result of having your music out there on sites with *millions* of visitors?

$100,000 last year? No?

How about $10,000 last year? Hmmm. . . . Goose eggs there too?

Did you even make $1,000?

The buzz is that it's a *great* time to be an independent artist. Not for you?

Guess what? You are not alone! Most people who press up 1,000 CDs never sell more than a couple *hundred*. And most of those people are doing all the same things you're doing—the MySpace, Twitter—all of it! And they aren't selling any music *either*.

C'mon, you *knew* this didn't you?

Then why have you joined the chorus of, "the major record labels suck?"

You might only get 15% of the gross, but wouldn't you rather have 15% of a record that sells a million units than 100% of nothing? Just sayin'!

"Indies are picking up a lot of acts that aren't going to fit on a major label in 2008, and releasing records from a lot of acts who, even five years ago, would have been on a major [label]."

Indie Labels Are Still Relevant

Hugh Leask

Hugh Leask is a senior reporter at Euromoney Institutional Investor. In the following viewpoint, he contends that hip hop music is facing declining music sales and fading popularity as a genre. Many music insiders blame major record labels for the current slump, he claims. While large record labels focus solely on the potential profitability of an artist, he argues that independent labels can offer artists the creative freedom and nourishment hip hop needs in order to be revitalized. He contends that while many major labels struggle to effectively market and promote their hip hop acts, Indie music labels still offer artists outside of the mainstream a chance to succeed. Indie labels, not major labels, Leask concludes, will give hip hop a fresh start.

As you read, consider the following questions:

1. What independent record company fostered hip hop stars such as Mos Def and Talib Kweli?

2. What are two reasons named by the author for the recent decline in hip hop sales?

3. Why, according to the viewpoint, would a major label never sign MF Doom?

At first glance, hip-hop circa 2008 seems a jaded and forlorn soul. Sure, its marquee names—Kanye West, 50 Cent, The Neptunes—still all eat well, but rap music as a whole has seen its mainstream profile eclipsed by a new crop of indie rock bands, a shift reflected in the much-quoted 20-plus per cent slump in sales of the genre between 2005 and 2006. Hip-hop's major record labels—once guaranteed sizeable returns at the cash registers from their star rosters—are feeling the pinch and have promptly slashed promotional budgets, cut staff and dropped artists.

A Struggling Genre

The music's current public face meanwhile is that of a bloated, stifled scene, crammed with materialistic MCs decked out in oversized sportswear whose lethargic lyrics have become as flat as last night's Cristal [champagne]. In short, things aren't too sweet.

But dig down deep enough, beyond the tales of pistols, pussy and the police, and you'll see there's a faint pulse still detectable within the recent output of many smaller, independent labels that don't usually land on mainstream radars. In March, hotly-tipped Detroit rhymeslinger Guilty Simpson, a protégé of late producer Jay Dee, released his debut album, *Ode to the Ghetto*—which was one of the most anticipated rap albums in years—on cult California label Stones Throw.

The buzz generated by Brooklyn-based imprint Nature Sounds in the last year reached fever pitch with must-have re-leases from Wu-Tang Clan rapper Masta Killa and more recently the legendary producer, DJ and one-time Nas and Public Enemy collaborator, Pete Rock.

And then there's UK-based Lex Records, which brought New York producer Danger Mouse—the brains behind the Jay-Z/Beatles mash-up *The Grey Album* and the gazillion-selling Gnarls Barkley—to mainstream attention. Later this year, the label will launch the latest project from US underground sensation MF Doom, whose mysterious metal mask and obscure pop culture-layered rhymes have brought him critical acclaim from far beyond the confines of the backpack-and-baggy-pants set.

Commercial vs. Underground Hip Hop

"I think that it's a good time for hip-hop in the sense that there's great music being made by artists all over the world," says Tom Brown, head of Lex, which is also known for its more eccentric, leftfield output such as Kid Acne and Boom Bip. "But it's a bad time commercially. Hip-hop is on the dark side of the moon as far as the media is concerned. Sooner or later things will change and all this terrible haircut indie rock will vanish—but until then we've just got to hang in there."

Sure, Brown's notion of a flourishing, creative underground music scene ignored and marginalized by the commercial sector is not confined to hip-hop, and yes, the idea of railing against corporatism in music is certainly nothing new. Hip-hop itself has been here before.

Around a decade ago, as Puff Daddy, Lil' Kim and others of their boastful, self-congratulating shiny-suited ilk were espousing their boozy, bling-bling agendas in clunky raps over chart-friendly re-heated disco hits—and clocking up sizeable amounts of record sales in the process—a small cluster of independent labels in New York sought to serve rap fans with a genuine alternative to the sugar-coated product peddled by the majors.

An independent-spirited and resolutely anti-commercial underground hip-hop movement of sorts was born, led by the famed Rawkus Records imprint. Rawkus would go on to foster future stars such as Mos Def and Talib Kweli, who won critical acclaim with politically charged work which spoke of self-empowerment and individualism. Inevitably, though, Rawkus—and other like-minded labels such as Fondle 'Em Records and Hydra Entertainment—would be gobbled up by the industry as hip-hop's march was steered in the direction of the dollar and it stormed the pop charts, making wealthy global superstars out of Jay-Z, Eminem and 50 Cent.

Today's Declining Music Sales

The difference now, of course, is that even the most glossy, glitzy commercial rap isn't shifting the kind of numbers it did in P Diddy's late-Nineties heyday. Stacks of column inches have focused on the spiraling trend of illegal downloads and their impact on the music industry, but within hip-hop circles many see the major labels' often ham-fisted approach to the music as another significant contributing factor to the current critical and commercial malaise.

Consider Jay-Z's tenure in charge of US giant [record label] Def Jam, arguably the biggest and most important label in rap history. When it appointed the New York rapper as president in late 2004, the move was widely hailed in the industry as a masterstroke. But very quickly, rumours were spreading about how Jay-Z's colossal ego was leading to other Def Jam artists' projects being sidelined and delayed. While rap fans were clamouring for new music from Def Jam stars Nas and Ghostface Killah, their release dates were constantly changed or inexplicably put back by execs behind the scenes.

"Being independent allows the label to be dynamic," says Tom Brown of the contrast between the major and indie strategies. "Indies can make quick decisions, and do much better deals with artists." He adds that despite the majors' larger budgets and a wider focus, they still lack the nous [understanding] of the indies when it comes to understanding maverick artists. "If you have a good person fighting your corner at a major label then you can have a long career. The problem is that staff changes over fairly rapidly at majors and if the guy in your corner gets fired in a cost-cutting exercise that might well mean that your album gets shelved or doesn't get the attention it needs.

"On-the-way-up artists such as Danger Mouse are huge creative talents and need the attention that an indie can give them. Later in an artist's career indies provide a creative environment," Brown continues, adding: "MF Doom's next solo project, under his DOOM moniker, will be on Lex. A major label would probably never sign DOOM directly because he's unlikely to deliver the pop success they need—but he is probably the most important creative force in hip-hop."

Independent Labels Benefit Artists

A quick scan of the hip-hop rosters on both indies and majors seems to reinforce the idea that up-and-coming rappers who sit outside the comfort zone of mainstream hip-hop—as well as legends of yesteryear considered past their sell-by-date by most majors—are finding creative nourishment on independent labels.

"Indies are picking up a lot of acts that aren't going to fit on a major label in 2008, and releasing records from a lot of acts who, even five years ago, would have been on a major," says Phillip Mlynar, deputy editor of *Hip-Hop Connection* magazine, about the current environment.

However, despite their taking a more grassroots approach and, some would argue, a greater risk on maverick artists, Mlynar reckons the cachet and air of authenticity that once surrounded independent rap labels like Rawkus has long since ebbed away.

"There's no championing of independent status by artists like there was during the mid-to-late Nineties," he says. "No one's coming out boasting about being independent—people just seem to accept that most rappers aren't going to be given a chance on a major label, so being on an indie is a natural fit, and possibly their only real option."

Yet for Brown, the current vitality within the indie hip-hop scene isn't simply by default in a climate where majors struggle to effectively market and promote their hip-hop acts. "I think indie labels work with artists who genuinely push the envelope," he adds. "Most indies will give an artist total creative freedom. So when indies 'push the envelope' it's really by giving the artists room to make amazing records."

> *"No other party comes close to the levels of investment committed by record companies to developing, nurturing and promoting talent."*

New Report Shows How Much Record Companies Are "Investing in Music"

IFPI

The International Federation of the Phonographic Industry (IFPI) is the organization that represents the interests of the recording industry worldwide. In the following viewpoint, IFPI argues that record companies and labels are vital for artists and for the music industry. IFPI says that record companies invest $5 billion a year in developing and promoting artists, which it contends is a very high rate of investment compared to other industries. IFPI argues that labels provide advances, tour support, money for videos, and other necessary investments.

As you read, consider the following questions:

1. How many artists does IFPI estimate are on major record labels and how many on independent labels?
2. According to the author, what is the typical cost of recording when breaking a new pop act in a major market?

3. What does IFPI estimate is the commercial success ratio of music artists?

- US$5 billion a year invested in artists by record companies worldwide
- Around 30% of revenues spent on artist development and marketing
- US$1 million to break a new artist in major markets
- US$160 billion "broader" sector employing two million people

Record companies, large and small, invest around US$5 billion a year in music talent, support a global roster of thousands of artists and typically spend US$1 million to break successful pop acts in major markets.

The figures are published in a new report issued highlighting the work of major and independent record companies as the principal investors in artists' careers. Advances, recording, marketing and promotional costs are the biggest items of record company spending on artists, commonly totalling six figure sums.

There are more than 4,000 artists on major record companies' rosters combined, and many thousands more on independent labels. There is continuous re-investment of revenues derived from successful acts into new talent. It is estimated that one in four artists on record companies' rosters were signed in the last 12 months.

Record companies are the largest investors in music talent, ploughing around 30% of their sales revenues—around US$5 billion worldwide—into developing and marketing artists. This includes an estimated 16% of sales revenues that is spent on artist and repertoire work (A&R), a proportion that significantly exceeds the proportionate research and development (R&D) expenditure of virtually all other industries. In addition, labels pay significant sums in royalties to featured performers.

Recorded music has a massive economic "ripple effect", helping generate a broader music sector, including live music, radio, publishing and audio equipment, estimated to be worth US$160 billion annually. IFPI estimates that more than two million people are employed globally in this broader music economy.

"Investing in Music" Report

Investing in Music is published by IFPI, representing the recording industry worldwide, in collaboration with WIN, the international network of independent record labels. The report provides new figures and outlines the special skills and services companies provide in developing and promoting artists.

Alison Wenham, Chair of AIM/WIN, says: "The direct route afforded by the internet is open to all. However, mixing the talents of business and creativity is often a minefield, with creativity often compromised by the challenges of running a business, which requires totally different skills. Artists generally prefer to leave the complex administration of a rights based business to someone else."

The report uses data from IFPI's member record companies and case studies from around the world, including David Guetta, Kasabian, Little Boots, Jason Mraz, Belanova, Mousse T and Stephane Pompougnac. Highlights include:

- A&R combines internet technology and traditional scouting skills, playing a critical role in bringing artists to a wide audience. Labels help their artists cut through the digital noise, with more than 2.5 million hip hop and 1.8 million rock acts registered on MySpace alone.
- Record labels invest increasingly through "broad rights" deals across different activities of an artist's work, including live and merchandising and branding. Multi-album deals are often important in allowing a return on this substantial investment. In many cases, artists and record labels enjoy long-term partnerships.

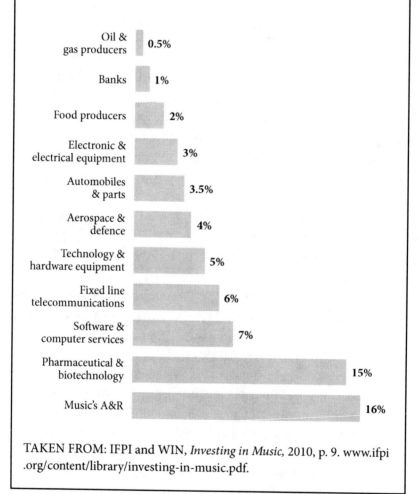

A Comparison of Up-front Investments

This graph compares the investment by the music industry in Artist and Repertoire with the investment by other sectors in Research and Development.

Sector	Percentage
Oil & gas producers	0.5%
Banks	1%
Food producers	2%
Electronic & electrical equipment	3%
Automobiles & parts	3.5%
Aerospace & defence	4%
Technology & hardware equipment	5%
Fixed line telecommunications	6%
Software & computer services	7%
Pharmaceutical & biotechnology	15%
Music's A&R	16%

TAKEN FROM: IFPI and WIN, *Investing in Music*, 2010, p. 9. www.ifpi .org/content/library/investing-in-music.pdf.

- The work in the studio to record the album and select the singles remains a very significant investment and area of collaboration.
- The marketing skills and resources of record companies,

from video production to online promotion, are essential in bringing artists to a mass audience. An international marketing "war machine" helps artists develop into global stars.

- Despite the success of the live music sector in recent years, recorded music remains the foundation for a successful artist career.

John Kennedy, chairman and chief executive of IFPI, says:

Investing in music is the core mission of record companies. No other party can lay claim to a comparable role in the music sector. No other party comes close to the levels of investment committed by record companies to developing, nurturing and promoting talent.

One of the biggest myths about the music industry in the digital age is that artists no longer need record labels. It is simply wrong. The investment, partnership and support that help build artist careers have never been more important than they are today. This report aims to explain why. Investing in Music is about how the music business works. It explains the value that music companies add, helping artists to realise a talent that would typically go unrecognised and get to an audience they would otherwise not reach.

Much of the value added by music companies is invisible to the outside world. Yet it is the investment and advice from labels that enable an artist to build a career in music and which, in turn, creates a beneficial ripple effect throughout the wider music sector.

High Levels of Investment

It is estimated that the recorded music industry spends around 30% of its total revenues—around US$5 billion a year—discovering, developing and promoting talent. Of that, a global average of 16% is spent on A&R, with a higher than average level in certain countries such as the UK (where A&R investment totalled 23% in 2007).

Global music industry investment in A&R is considerably higher than similar investments in other industries. In the UK, the pharmaceutical and biotechnology industry, widely acknowledged as a leader in research and development, invests 15% of its gross revenues in R&D (BIS R&D Scoreboard, 2008).

A&R spending today, however, is under greater pressure than ever from the impact of illegal file-sharing and other forms of piracy. In France, industry data shows record companies invested 12% of their turnover in marketing artists in 2009, a proportion that fell from 15% in 2006, at a time of reduced revenues which have been largely attributed to illegal file-sharing.

How the Investment Breaks Down

Investing in Music outlines the very substantial investments involved in developing and marketing successful artists. In the UK and US it is estimated that it typically costs more than US$1 million to break a pop artist. This is spread across an advance paid to the artist, recording costs, video production, tour support and promotional work. A typical example of the breakdown of the costs of breaking a new pop act in major markets is as below:

Advance	US$200,000
Recording	US$200,000
3 videos	US$200,000
Tour support	US$100,000
Promotion/marketing	US$300,000
TOTAL	US$1,000,000

- *Payment of an advance to the artist.* Such an advance allows an artist to give up their day job and concentrate on writing, rehearsing, recording and performing music. Advances are recoupable from an artist's sales, but are not recouped if those sales do not reach certain levels, leaving the record company bearing the risk of investment. A typical advance paid to a new pop act in major markets is US$200,000, but often will be higher. Advances for an established "superstar" act will commonly be in excess of US$1 million.

- *Financing of recording costs.* Costs could be over US$200,000 for a new artist to record an album, though employing a top producer can drive this above US$50,000 per track. Hiring large numbers of session musicians or an orchestra can also drive up the budget. In this way, investment in recordings benefits a wide community of musicians and technicians.

- *Production of videos.* Video costs can also range widely. Some of the most expensive ever produced involved days of filming and editing, costing around $1 million. A typical cost for filming videos to promote a new artist's album is around US$200,000.

- *Tour support.* New artists in particular need to be heavily supported by record companies. The level of tour support required is highly dependent on the nature of the artist. Tour support would typically cost around US$100,000 for a new artist in one market.

- *Marketing and promotion.* These are often the biggest budget items for a record label taking an act to the public. Labels invest heavily in marketing and promoting artists to a broad audience. Such promotion builds the brand identity from which artists can then earn money from numerous sources, such as live touring or merchandise. A typical investment in marketing and promoting a new act is US$300,000.

- *Royalty payments.* Payment of royalties is usually based on a percentage of revenues, licensed or synchronised income revenue streams. Teams in music companies are responsible for collecting and distributing royalties to the featured performers, producers and copyright owners.

The Virtuous "Circle of Investment"

Recording contracts typically commit artists and labels to work together to produce a series of albums. Artists benefit from heavy upfront investment that would be difficult to secure elsewhere and record labels have the opportunity to recoup their outlay over a period of time.

Achieving commercial hits is the basis of the "circle of investment", by which music companies plough back the revenues generated by successful campaigns to develop new talent and help fund the next generation of artists.

Continually investing in new talent is a hugely risky business, as only a minority of the artists developed by music companies will be commercially successful in a highly competitive market. Estimates on the commercial success ratio of artists vary between one in five and one in ten.

The level of investment in new artists required remains high, despite the development of new distribution channels for recorded music. In fact, the fragmentation of music distribution across many different physical and digital channels has often brought extra costs to record companies that are now working with many more retail partners.

"*After suing [a file-sharing service that does not pay artists, Sony is] acting just like them by not paying the artists.*"

Behind the Music: The Real Reason Why the Major Labels Love Spotify

Helienne Lindvall

Helienne Lindvall is a professional songwriter and musician; she writes regularly for the Guardian, *a major British newspaper. In the following viewpoint she reports on Spotify, a UK company that streams music online. Lindvall says that Spotify has made deals to compensate major labels for the use of their catalogues, but that these deals provide little revenue for artists. Lindvall argues that the labels and Spotify need to pay artists fair rates for the use of their music.*

As you read, consider the following questions:

1. Why does Lindvall say she was worried about the small number of advertisements on Spotify?
2. What does the author say Spotify is valued at (as of August 2009) and how does this compare to its income?
3. Who is Magnus Uggla, and why did he pull his music from Spotify, according to Lindvall?

No wonder the majors speak so highly of Spotify—they receive 18%
of shares in the online streaming service. It's just a pity that artists
won't get to see any of this.

The launch of Spotify in the UK must surely be one of the biggest PR successes for an online music service. Despite only having spent around £5,000 on marketing since 2006 (according to Daniel Ek, one of Spotify's founders), they've managed to gain huge media coverage—not least in *The Guardian*.

It's been described as sexy, incredibly user-friendly and the future—maybe even the saviour—of legal music consumption. I've met Ek, a fellow Swede. He seemed like a really nice guy who loves music, and when he said it's important that artists are compensated, I really wanted Spotify to be all the things the hype had promised.

I signed up and quickly realised that, yes, Spotify is indeed user-friendly—if not for discovering new music, for rediscovering music from my teenage years as well as records I've lost along the way. But I wondered how artists could be compensated with so few adverts (sometimes, despite being logged on for hours, I haven't seen any ads at all). As more details about their operation have emerged, my initial choice to put them in my proposed Fair Trade category appears to have been a bit premature.

The major record labels—and the bigger indies—that I spoke to seemed unusually positive about Spotify, which made me think that they must have received a pretty hefty payment and/or equity in the company. Sure enough, the other week some of my suspicions were confirmed when it was reported that the majors received 18% of Spotify shares. Merlin, who represents a large portion of the independent labels, received 1% (as their labels represent 11–12% of Spotify plays, it appears this is a bit disproportionate to the value of their content). What they paid for their shares is still under debate, with ComputerSweden reporting that it was as little as $10,000. Regarding payments, the labels I spoke to said that they're not allowed to divulge these details. But, as it's common for majors to demand such payments, I'd say it's likely they did.

I can see why this puts Spotify in their good books. One of the main reasons why majors have been hesitant to offer their music to start-ups is that they've seen companies like YouTube and Last.fm build businesses, only to sell them off for big bucks without sharing the money with the copyright owners whose music they used.

A source close to Spotify told me he has serious doubts that their business model will add up and that it's a case of "spot the idiot", i.e., "find somebody stupid enough to buy it before realising that it's too costly to run and that the numbers don't add up to making a profit".

Spotify is currently valued at $250m, despite, according to *The Register*, only having an advertising income of £82,000 and just 17,000 UK users signing up to pay £120 a year for Spotify Premium. Having equity in the company ensures that the labels get paid if Ek and his colleagues find said "idiot" and decide to sell up (Ek says they have no intention of selling up, by the way). But what does this all mean for the artists?

On Spotify, it seems, artists are not equal. There are indie labels that, as opposed to the majors and Merlin members, receive no advance, receive no minimum per stream and only get a 50% share of ad revenue on a pro-rata basis (which so far has amounted to next to nothing). Incidentally, when I asked a Spotify rep if they would feature music by unsigned artists the way We7 does, he said no, but that all they would need to do was to sign up to a label and they'd get on the site.

For artists who "signed up to a label" there's a tangible risk that revenue which comes from a possible sale of shares by the label would end up in the proverbial "blackbox" (non-attributable revenue that remains with the label). There's growing concern about this in the artist management community and, a few weeks ago, Bob Dylan decided to pull his back catalogue from UK streaming services. The only Dylan albums currently on Spotify are Bob Dylan's 60s Live, A 30th Anniversary Concert Celebration, a tribute compilation and a few tracks that are featured on movie soundtracks.

In Sweden, where Spotify has been running the longest, Magnus Uggla—well-established since the late 70s—has withdrawn his music from the service. On his blog he said that, after six months on the site he'd earned "what a mediocre busker could earn in a day". Regarding his record label, Sony Music, he says "after suing the shit out of Pirate Bay, they're acting just like them by not paying the artists". When he found out that Sony had 5.8% equity in Spotify he wrote: "I would rather be raped by Pirate Bay than f---ed up the ass by (Sony boss) Hasse Breitholtz and Sony Music and will remove all of my songs from Spotify pending an honest service."

As labels taking equity in new services becomes commonplace (the majors are currently in the process of doing it with BskyB and VirginMedia for their soon-to-be-launched music services), the issue of how to compensate the artist is a problem that won't go away and needs to be resolved.

So, in the light of recent revelations, I'm afraid I'm going to have to withdraw the virtual Fair Trade stamp I gave Spotify a few months back, until they prove that they are, indeed, concerned about treating artists right.

Periodical and Internet Sources Bibliography

The following articles have been selected to supplement the diverse views presented in this chapter.

Charles Arthur	"Spotify's Limits on Free Use Will Please the Big Record Labels," *Guardian* (Manchester, UK), April 14, 2011.
Elisa Bray	"The Beauty of Being an Independent Record Label," *Independent* (London), July 3, 2009.
Carrie Brownstein	"Roundtable Discussions: The Role of the Record Label," NPR Online, November 16, 2009. www.npr.org.
Chris Castle	"An Inconvenient Truth: Songwriters Guild President Rick Carnes Talks About the Effect of Piracy on American Songwriters," NJN Network, February 4, 2009.
Jason Feinberg	"What Will Record Labels Look Like in the Future?," PBS MediaShift, August 18, 2009. www.pbs.org.
Mike Masnick	"Forget Infringement, Major Labels Should Be Worrying About Having to Pay Much Higher Royalties on Downloads," TechDirt, March 23, 2011. www.techdirt.com.
Andrew Orlowski	"Big Label Stakes Highlight Spotify's Truthiness Trouble," The Register, August 7, 2009. www.theregister.co.uk.
Timothy Quirk	"My Hilarious Warner Bros. Royalty Statement," Too Much Joy, December 1, 2009. www.toomuchjoy.com.
Wayne Rosso	"Warner Music: The Pillaging of a Once Great Record Company," The Music Void, February 24, 2011. www.themusicvoid.com.

Will Changes in the Industry Hurt Music?

Chapter Preface

The music industry has changed radically over the last fifty years. Videos have become essential for the promotion of big stars. Digital production techniques have made it possible to radically change the sound of a singer's voice on a record, or even in performance. Changes in distribution have altered the way that consumers find and interact with music.

Have all of these changes benefited the music itself? Or have the changes hurt music?

Many people argue that the changes have hurt. David Bauder, writing in a February 2, 2006, article in *USA Today*, for example, reported on a poll that said that 58 percent of music fans "complain that music in general is getting worse." Rap music was particularly controversial; hip hop was the favorite style of music among 18 percent of fans under age thirty-five, and the favorite of only 2 percent of those over thirty-five. But even 49 percent of younger fans aged eighteen to thirty-four in the poll said that music "is getting worse."

Some people complain because music lyrics are too crude or violent, or because singers aren't as talented as they used to be. A writer of an August 10, 2010, post on the *Musicouch* blog argued that contemporary "music is abnormal[l]y simple, and it's not the beautiful simple like so many Beatles song[s]. It is annoying synths that are so common that I usually can easily predict the rest of the song from the first 30 seconds."

Music definitely has changed in some ways. For instance, Cliff Kuang writing at *Fast Company* reports that pop song volumes have been getting steadily louder over time, because "Sound engineers are tinkering with songs to make them stand out on the radio and on MP3s."

However, music critic Neil McCormick argues that it is not really that pop music is getting worse so much as that people *always* believe pop music is getting worse. Writing in a June 20,

2002, article in London's *Daily Telegraph*, McCormick said that people tend to get "stuck in a rut" with their music listening. Most listeners interact with music most intently when they are younger. As they get older, their listening becomes more casual and less adventurous. McCormick says that "given its relative importance in their social and cultural life, young people (like music critics) tend to be willing to put in the time and summon the genuine effort sometimes required to crack musical codes and find the key that unlocks each new genre." Older people, he says, are less interested in putting in the effort, and tend to gravitate to "things that sound familiar."

The following viewpoints consider how various recent innovations in the music industry have, or have not, affected the quality of music.

> *"Today there are few, if any, examples of true recording artists left."*

The Reduced Focus on Recording Is a Loss to Music

Rick Carnes

Rick Carnes is the president of the Songwriting Guild of America. In the following viewpoint he argues that digital piracy has made it unprofitable for musicians to focus on recordings. Instead, he says, musicians have to concentrate on live performances and merchandising. As a result, he argues, song quality has fallen. He concludes that the golden age of American songwriting is over and laments the fact that recordings such as those made by the Beatles are no longer possible.

As you read, consider the following questions:

1. What does Carnes say has replaced the big recording studios and studio musicians?
2. Why, according to the author, was Stephen Foster forced to write for minstrel shows?
3. According to Carnes, what should music do rather than simply catch the eye?

After their world tour in 1966, The Beatles quit touring as a group.

The interviews have stated that they were tired of trying to perform when they couldn't hear themselves over the screaming audience and were increasingly interested in producing more progressive and experimental music in the recording studio.

The recent release of The Beatles' catalog by [digital download store] iTunes has given the public a chance to revisit a period of pop music in which each new Beatles album was a potential advance in the art of recorded pop music. The Beatles were constantly searching for new sounds and new techniques that would deliver their songs in innovative ways to an audience that was eager to hear the newest sounds on the best audio equipment they could afford.

Album sales allowed The Beatles to retire from touring and devote themselves full time to writing and recording. By focusing on albums as a unified musical statement in "Sgt. Pepper's Lonely Hearts Club Band" and "Abbey Road," The Beatles raised the bar for all the albums that followed and changed recording quality and technique worldwide. They also helped launch the Album Oriented Rock radio format and spawned a rash of 'concept' albums that continued into the 1990's.

The Beatles, by abandoning touring and focusing instead on writing, recording, and selling albums, invented the "Recording Artist."

Today there are few, if any, examples of true recording artists left. In the digital age of music when we listen to severely compressed recordings through tiny earphones, the quest for better fidelity is quixotic at best and a complete waste of money at worst. The big recording studios are quickly fading into the past and the studio musicians who were able to devote their lives to improving their sound and their technique are a dying breed, replaced by home recording studios and sample-looping software.

Albums Are an Afterthought

Today's music artist is focused on image and brand development because the money is made on ticket sales for live shows. Album sales are an after thought since music piracy has obliterated the ability to support an act through recorded music sales alone. Recorded music is given away as a promotional loss-leader, sold as an adjunct to a new tech device, or as an impulse buy at big discount stores. Gone are the record stores of old.

Damian Kulash of the group OK Go said it best in a *Wall Street Journal* article about the "New Rock Star Paradigm", "We're just moving out of the brief period—a flash in history's pan—when an artist could expect to make a living selling records alone." He touts the fact that his band has prospered by leaping across treadmills, dancing with a dozen dogs and building the world's largest Rube Goldberg machine[1] to operate in time with music all captured on video to promote the live performance, licensing, and sponsorship opportunities of his band. Oh yes, and you can buy their recordings as well, but they are not the focus of the band. Nor could they be. It takes a *lot* of time, energy and creativity to do the videos they do. Why devote that time to the largely unprofitable enterprise of focusing on the writing and recording of the music? In Kulash's new paradigm the recording is free goods to get fans to come to the live show and buy the T-shirts. Obviously, his band is focusing on the only revenue streams that piracy has left them. That's smart on the one hand, but sad on the other.

If music piracy continues unabated I am certain that Kulash's vision of the future of the music business will prove correct. The reason I am certain is that this is not the future of music, it is the ugly past repeating itself.

A Shining Moment

In the 19th century, British, Scottish, and Irish music were not protected by US copyright law. This led to US songwriters having to compete with a flood of free music coming in from overseas.

Stephen Foster and "Oh! Susanna"

Foster knew what it was like for a song to go viral [that is, become popular and much-duplicated] and escape from his control. He had inadvertently allowed his first hit "Oh! Susanna" to slip into the public domain by sending out manuscript copies before it was copyrighted. At least 20 different publishers brought out their own editions of the song; only one of them paid for the rights. This was perfectly legal in 1849.

Barry Alfonso, Pittsburgh Post-Gazette,
April 25, 2010.

Our native-born composers like Stephen Foster were reduced to writing the only type of music that the British weren't producing, i.e. minstrel songs. The traveling minstrel show was the only place that Foster could eke out a few dollars. The focus of the Minstrel shows was most definitely not the music but the comedy show instead, mostly racist in content. History shows that Foster did not enjoy writing this type of music and was capable, when given the opportunity, of writing much better work. But it wasn't until 1909 and the new US Copyright Act, that protected the work of foreign writers, that US songwriters no longer had to "compete with free." This led to an explosion of new songs in what we now refer to as the Golden Age of American songwriting. Damian refers to it dismissively as a "flash in history's pan," but as a songwriter I prefer to think of it as a shining moment when great American music captured the imagination of the world.

But now widespread theft of music has returned to wipe out the creative and financial gains made by 20th-century songwriters and artists, and as Damian points out, "Without records as clearly delineated receptacles of value, last century's rules—both industrial and creative—are out the window." The incentive is no longer there for creating a great recording. The money, just like in the Minstrel days, is now in putting on a show.

We can all see that future every time we watch the music videos on YouTube. But music can, and should, do more than simply catch the eye—it should please the ear and hopefully move the soul as well.

After hearing The Beatles again last month I was reminded of a time when the songs mattered more and great recorded sound was the focus. I remembered what it was like when records were indeed "receptacles of value." And for a brief, luminous moment I leaned back in my chair, closed my eyes, and enjoyed receiving some very extraordinary value.

Note

1. A Rube Goldberg machine is any absurdly complicated machine for performing a simple task.

> *"There are plenty of examples of studio acts that produce amazing studio music and do a ton of touring."*

Musicians Will Continue to Record Great Music

Tim Geigner

Tim Geigner (also known as Dark Helmet) is a regular writer for the website Techdirt. In the following viewpoint, he argues that the prevalence of digital piracy will not hurt recorded music. He says that most musicians have always toured and recorded and that that will continue. He also notes that cheaper recording technology has made it easier for musicians to record without the expense of a major studio. He concludes that there is reason for optimism, not pessimism, about the future of recorded music.

As you read, consider the following questions:

1. According to Geigner, during what period did the Beatles tour?
2. Why does the author say that smaller recording operations are springing up, and why does he not believe it is related to a fall in quality?
3. What cultural benefit does Geigner see as resulting from the lack of copyright before 1909?

Tim Geigner, "Music Piracy = The Death of the Recording Artist," TechDirt.com, January 5, 2011. Reproduced by permission.

Mike [Masnick, CEO and founder of Techdirt] did a post at the end of 2010 talking about moving forward optimistically with our views and expectations of music, movies and media. It's kind of interesting to see the difference in approach between those on either side of the same old debates being had about the subject and how that approach is reflected in people's thoughts and language.

Unnecessary Pessimism

Which brings me to a recent piece by Rick Carnes, President of the Songwriters Guild of America, for the *Huffington Post*. He asks if music piracy has killed the recording artist. Rick has been discussed at Techdirt in the past, such as when he made some seemingly misguided comments on maximizing per-use revenue with regard to iTunes previews rather than what maximizes overall revenue, or that the internet is making it impossible to write music and has "destroyed the profession of songwriting". These are pessimistic words and thoughts. And in his latest article, there is more pessimism that really needs to be addressed.

Rick discusses his fondness for The Beatles and some of the amazing things they did for music and experimental recording techniques. He then goes on to suggest that the reason The Beatles were able to do that type of thing was largely because they stopped touring and could focus their efforts in the studio instead. For the younger crowd, it might surprise you, as it did me, to find out that The Beatles did so little actual touring that, on the whole, they would have to be considered a studio act, not a live act. Basically, they toured between 1962 and 1966, and that's about it. Guess what time period is labeled "Beatlemania". Yup, during their touring years. Why is that important? Because of some of the things Rick says in his piece.

> Today there are few, if any, examples of true recording artists left. . . . The big recording studios are quickly fading into the past and the studio musicians who were able to devote their

Advice for Musicians Interested in Recording

If you're like most musicians, you've been noodling around on your instrument for a while and have finally decided to take the plunge and get serious about recording your ideas. You may just want to throw a few ideas down onto tape (or hard drive) or capture those magic moments that you have with your band. Or you may want to compose, record, produce, and release the next great platinum album. Either way, you'll find that having a home studio can give you hours of satisfaction.

Well, you've chosen a great time to get involved in audio recording. Not long ago, you needed to go to a commercial recording studio and spend thousands of dollars if you wanted to make a decent-sounding recording. Now you can set up a first-class recording studio in your garage or spare bedroom and create CDs that can sound as good as those coming out of top-notch studios (that is, if you know how to use the gear).

Jeff Strong, Home Recording for Musicians for Dummies, *2009.*

lives to improving their sound and their technique are a dying breed, replaced by home recording studios and sample-looping software.

I don't see how this makes sense. There are plenty of recording artists around today. But besides that, there's a ton of recorded music being produced. And the reason you're seeing smaller operations spring up to provide studio-style recordings isn't because listeners don't care about quality. It's because the difference in quality has been rendered negligible by advances in technology. This is a *good* thing for music lovers, because barriers are coming down. I think that perhaps if Rick could see this from the perspective of the music fan, he'd see it that way as well.

> Album sales are an after thought since music piracy has obliterated the ability to support an act through recorded music sales alone. Recorded music is given away as a promotional loss-leader, sold as an adjunct to a new tech device, or as an impulse buy at big discount stores.

The Beatles Were Different

To be fair, if we're only comparing The Beatles to everyone else today, Rick probably has a point. But that's a silly comparison. The Beatles are the best-selling musical act of all time, according to many sources. But, even in its most profitable time, were album sales really supporting any significant percentage of the musical acts around? Through the wonder of music label accounting, even in the 60's, music acts were rarely able to make it on record sales alone. And I think if Rick can get away from The Beatles example for a moment, he already knows this to be true. If it weren't, why would it be such an anomaly that most bands couldn't stop touring the way The Beatles did? I'm just not sure things were ever the way Rick says they were. And then there's this.

> In the 19th century, British, Scottish, and Irish music were not protected by US copyright law. This led to US songwriters having to compete with a flood of free music coming in from overseas. Our native-born composers like Stephen Foster were reduced to writing the only type of music that the British weren't producing, i.e. minstrel songs. The traveling minstrel show was the only place that Foster could eke out a few dollars. The focus of the Minstrel shows was most definitely not the music but the comedy show instead, mostly racist in content. . . . It wasn't until 1909 and the new US Copyright Act,

that protected the work of foreign writers, that US songwriters no longer had to "compete with free.

Ugh. If I'm reading his allusion correctly, I see two astounding claims here. First, The Copyright Act of 1909 was responsible for the obliteration of a great deal of racist comedy in the United States. Secondly, if piracy continues, that racist comedy is going to come back. He can't really mean that, can he?

And I'm a little fuzzy on the logic here as well. You had music lovers in the United States that were being "flooded" with music from overseas. Ostensibly, this is music they wanted, because it was being consumed. So, basically, Rick is saying that less copyright led to a flood of musical output. Wouldn't that be a cultural benefit? But then, in 1909 with the Copyright Act, that flood was stymied and United States musicians were better off . . . because foreign music was protected? Doesn't that seem to suggest that copyright was used as some kind of import levy?

In any case, I don't think Rick should be as concerned as he is. There are plenty of examples of musical acts that produce amazing studio music *and* do a ton of touring (The Rolling Stones, anyone?). I recognize that some of this may be political posturing as Rick tries to appease his base constituents of songwriters but perhaps with a little less rhetoric and a little more discussion, we'll all find ourselves in a better place at the end of 2011 compared to the beginning.

> *"Still, the court determined that the contract clause was designed to allow the group to 'preserve the artistic integrity of the albums."'*

Some Artists Feel that Downloading of Single Tracks Destroys the Integrity of an Album

Peter Lauria

Peter Lauria is a reporter who has covered US media, entertainment, and technology for Reuters, the Daily Beast, *and the* New York Post. *In the following viewpoint, Lauria reports on the outcome of the lawsuit filed by the rock group Pink Floyd against the record label company EMI. The court found in favor of the band's position that a clause in the contract prohibited sale of individual songs in digital format from select albums, not just in physical format sales, which was the record label company's position. Though the band reserves the right to sell songs individually, they also won the right to treat their albums as artistic wholes.*

As you read, consider the following questions:

1. From which albums did Pink Floyd want to prevent EMI's selling of individual tracks?
2. Under what conditions can EMI sell individual songs from Pink Floyd albums?
3. How did Pink Floyd market its songs for CBS' "Cold Case"?

The hits keep coming for record label EMI.

A British court yesterday [March 11, 2010] ruled in favor of Pink Floyd, bringing to a close the acid rock band's lawsuit seeking to prohibit EMI from selling individual tracks from its albums online.

The ruling came just a day after the resignation of CEO Elio Leoni-Sceti, amid internal turmoil over a strategic plan to be presented to investors in Guy Hands-owned [investment firm] Terra Firma.

Pink Floyd's lawsuit dates back to last April, when the band asked the court for its interpretation on a clause in its contract that "expressly prohibited" EMI from unbundling tracks from albums like *Dark Side of the Moon* and *The Wall*.

The judge disagreed with the label's position that the clause only applied to physical sales and not digital tracks. EMI was also ordered to cover the band's legal costs.

The impact of the ruling remains unclear, however. EMI can still sell individual Pink Floyd songs online with the band's written consent, which it can seek on a case-by-case basis. It can also cut a big check in return for blanket permission to sell singles in new formats.

Pink Floyd doesn't seem to be against new ways of marketing its back catalog, which is consistently among the best selling in music. An upcoming episode of CBS' *Cold Case*, for instance, includes seven songs.

Still, the court determined that the contract clause was designed to allow the group to "preserve the artistic integrity of the albums."

> "People are getting used to being the ones finally in control of how they buy and listen to their music and the simple fact is that they aren't going to pay for garbage tunes anymore."

Good Riddance to Albums

Steven Hodson

Steven Hodson blogs about technology issues at sites such as WinExtra and Mashable. In the following viewpoint, he argues that the album format no longer provides good value for the money. Most albums, he says, have only two or three good tracks, and the rest is filler. He argues that the downloadable single format allows listeners to buy only what they want. If artists and labels want listeners to start buying albums again, he contends, they need to start releasing higher-quality albums.

As you read, consider the following questions:
1. What albums does Hodson say were among the first he bought?

2. According to the author, why did people feel that the record companies had been stealing from them for years?

3. What does Hodson say will happen if record companies push hard for a return to the album format with only two or three songs worth paying for?

One of my fondest memories as a kid was saving up my money and making the trip to the record store where I would spend what seemed like hours going through the LP bins. Finally, I would narrow down my selection to what money I had in my pocket. Sometimes I would be able to get only one album, maybe two or on those rare occasions when there was a sale going on I'd get more. I can still remember the very first album that I bought was *YesSongs* by Yes, which was followed a couple weeks later by a purchase of *Brain Salad Surgery* by Emerson, Lake and Palmer.

Even though the 45 singles market was the most popular way to get the current hit albums, over the years I amassed quite the collection; especially of specialty colored vinyl pressings. Sure albums were more expensive, but at that time the quality of music being produced generally meant the majority of the album would be stuff that you liked. In the majority of cases there might be one or two songs on the album that you might not like, so the price we paid seemed to be a fair exchange.

As the years passed and vinyl changed to cassettes, which then changed to CDs, that fair exchange of money for quality music began to shift. Eventually it got to the point where you were lucky if there were two or three songs on that CD that you just paid $20.00 for [that] were any good. During this time along came the Internet and ways to convert those CDs into single files that could be played on any computer. People began to discover that no longer were they having to buy a whole CD to have only the good songs from it. They also found ways to be able to share all those songs with people around the world.

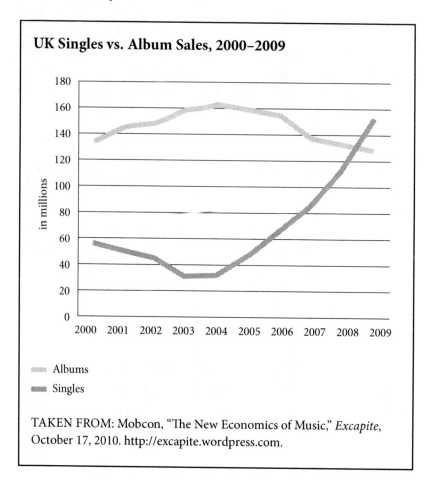

UK Singles vs. Album Sales, 2000–2009

Albums

Singles

TAKEN FROM: Mobcon, "The New Economics of Music," *Excapite*, October 17, 2010. http://excapite.wordpress.com.

It didn't matter if it was legal or not to a great many of these people because they felt—right or wrong—that the record companies had been stealing from them for years. After all, weren't the musicians themselves saying that they made next to no money from CD sales? It was their record companies who were really making all the money. Into this fray then came Apple and their iTunes store with the radical idea of selling single songs for 99¢ and in short order it became almost the defacto standard for buying legal music on the Internet.

Music distribution had changed, and for a change the people had the ability to buy exactly what they wanted for a fair price without being forced to pay extra for garbage tracks. The album concept was slowly losing ground and once more the single track, the modern day equivalent of the 45, was the most popular way of buying your music.

For some musicians though, this wasn't what they wanted and while some quite justly felt it ruined the musical experience they were trying to provide throughout the CD as a whole, for others it was all about the money. Or is it really the musicians that are concerned about this in the end—after all, aren't they the ones trying to tell us all that they don't make any money from CD sales?

While some big bands have shown that it is still possible to produce quality CDs that are meant to be listened to as a whole and that people will buy, the majority of musicians still only produce one or two good songs per CD. It is in cases like this where in my opinion the album CD concept is just a con job from the record companies to make us spend more money for less quality. This is why some record companies are pulling songs from iTunes under the pretense of artistic merit so that they can return to the album CD model and the larger dollar figures they make from it.

Unfortunately, those same record companies risk further damaging both their incomes and the artists' incomes by forcing this issue the way they are. The single track genie is out of the bottle and there is no way that it is going to go back in. People are getting used to being the ones finally in control of how they buy and listen to their music and the simple fact is that they aren't going to pay for garbage tunes anymore. If the record companies push hard for a return to the album CD with only one, two or maybe three songs worth paying for, people will give them the middle finger and return to the P2P networks in droves.

Using the argument that artists deserved to be paid for their work is partially correct. What is correct is that *the artists*—not the record labels—are the ones who deserve the lion's share of the income. That comes with a caveat though—they only deserve the money if the product is worth what you are charging for it.

At one time the album model worked, giving you the best value for your money, but that is no longer true in the vast majority of cases. As with the 45, the single tracks today are the customers' best value and if the musicians want to make more money then they need to start producing better music and less garbage.

The day of the album is gone unless musicians provide enough value for fans so that they are willing to pay for an album format. If not, the single track is what we will be buying for a very long time to come. It's up to musicians.

> "The music industry has been charting
> the decline of the classical market in the
> United States for at least a decade."

The Classical Music Market Is Collapsing

Michael Johnson

Michael Johnson is a writer and former editor at publishers McGraw-Hill. In the following viewpoint he reports that the classical music industry is imploding. City orchestras across America are closing as donations fall and interest in classical music wanes. Illegal downloading has also had a devastating effect on classical music sales, Johnson says. He reports that classical music is also struggling in Europe, though the situation is not as dire there as in the United States. Johnson notes that Asia is the one exception, as classical music training and performance are still highly valued there.

As you read, consider the following questions:

1. What symphonies does Johnson say are in dire financial difficulties?
2. Why has the Detroit orchestra been shut down since October 2010, according to the author?

3. According to Johnson, what factor has helped London do better than America in terms of maintaining viable symphonies?

The music industry has been charting the decline of the classical market in the United States for at least a decade, attributing it to aging audiences, crashing CD sales and shrinking private subsidies. Music lovers beware: there are signs now of an accelerating downward trend.

End of an Era

The root of the problem, musicians tell me, is a plague of pirated Internet downloads and a spreading anti-intellectual climate in the U.S. music world, especially among the young. Further pressure, as if any were needed, comes from the current economic squeeze.

Several of the nation's leading symphonies are wholly dependent on private donations. As the recession has taken hold, Detroit, Philadelphia, Cleveland and Pittsburgh orchestras are in dire financial difficulty, and [the] Louisville [Orchestra] filed for Chapter 11 bankruptcy protection. The Honolulu Symphony, the oldest orchestra west of the Rockies, went broke and shut down in December [2010]. In music-mad New York, many second-tier orchestras, including the Brooklyn Philharmonic and Long Island Philharmonic have stopped performing and others are downsizing, curtailing their season and asking players to take salary cuts.

Highly trained instrumentalists complain that the demand for their services is eroding year by year as job opportunities evaporate. Moreover, the arrival of Chinese, Korean and Japanese virtuosos from the top U.S. conservatories has heated up the competition both for permanent and freelance work.

It looks like a perfect storm has hit the business of serious music, so far sparing only the major orchestras in New York, Boston, Chicago and a few other cities. Some say they see an end of an era coming.

"It's a tough time for great music," says Melinda Bargreen, a composer and former *Seattle Times* critic who was recently sacked in a cost-cutting campaign at the newspaper.

The *New York Times* has called it the Classical Music Recession. This time, however, the recovery may come too late for city-based orchestras and players throughout the country.

It is already too late for some. A typical case is a professional cellist in New York who has seen his income plunge by two-thirds, forcing him to sell his home to feed his family and stay solvent. Another musician, a New York percussionist, has gone public with his plight, calling his once-busy life now haunted with "long stretches of quiet."

Even light-hearted classical concerts such as Peter Schickele's P.D.Q. Bach have stopped, not for quality reasons but because dumbed-down audiences miss his wisecracks due to poor musical knowledge.

Pervasive Ignorance

A pianist friend, Ivan Ilic, says the pervasive public ignorance of serious music has been a major factor in the current crisis. "It is naive to pretend that people will spontaneously flock to concerts because, say, the harmonic progressions are worked out in more detail in a [Franz] Schubert symphony than those in a song by Lady Gaga."

People need context to understand the music, he believes, "and the older the music the richer the context."

Reaction from residents of the cities worst affected has sparked emotional debates on the Internet over how much subsidy makes sense when audiences and benefactors are turning away. Many residents favor market forces as the main indicator in deciding whether an orchestra deserves to survive. In Detroit, where a crippling strike over wages has shut down the orchestra since last October [2010], one local reader wrote to the *Free Press* website: "Given the high (too high, actually) ticket prices for the DSO [Detroit Symphony Orchestra] and those high salaries for what basically is part-of-the-year work, I have almost zero sympathy for a symphony that has more or less struck itself out of a job."

Wrote another reader: "I don't need an orchestra in town and apparently I am not alone, otherwise enough paying customers would attend. The DSO loses money. It is not a compelling value proposition in the competition for the entertainment dollar of enough metro Detroiters to justify its survival. Take the pay cut, or shut it down. Simple as that."

In Louisville, a *Courier-Journal* reader commented: "Either community support exists or it doesn't. In this case, clearly the community support for an orchestra of this size doesn't exist and the LO [Louisville Orchestra] should reorganize into a sustainable entity."

As bloggers continued opting for a shutdown, one reader asked, "Tell me dear sir, what is the color of your neck?"

Problems Overseas

France and Germany have largely avoided U.S. problems, supporting their leading orchestras mainly through government subsidies. In Italy, however, opera companies and orchestras are both suffering. In Britain, subsidies are under pressure by cutbacks in government spending but an innovative economic model helps them survive.

London, arguably the music capital of the world, "is doing pretty well," says leading British music critic and writer Jessica Duchen, partly by "paying their players one heck of a lot less than the Americans do—possibly a quarter as much." The most successful orchestras—the London Symphony, London Philharmonic and Philharmonia—do not give full-time salaries. Players are paid on a freelance basis.

Ms. Bargreen laments the disappearance of the music critic from many U.S. newspapers. "What was lost was not only the continued vigilance and critical attention to this field," she told me, "but also the ability of classical performers to get their story out in a way that got more considered attention than the millions of tiny voices shouting into cyberspace."

The survival of orchestras has hit players' private finances in other ways, too. Demand for private lessons, which normally supplement their incomes, is dropping off as schools cut back music education and the entertainment industry floods the young with other options. One classically trained music teacher in Britain told me he has been forced to learn, and teach, the electric guitar to keep his job. Youngsters are not opting for his music appreciation courses.

Music lessons in British schools are expected to be chopped further as the government seeks to privatize this side of education. "It's as if, rather than just pruning the tree at sensible points of the branches, they want to pull it up by the roots," says Ms. Duchen.

And finally, the once-ubiquitous CD, which started losing market share about ten years ago, continues to fall in all categories. "The demand that everything on the Internet be free has meant that the vast majority of music downloads are illegal, thus depriving performers and composers of their deserved income," says composer-critic Bargreen.

Only in Asia is the classical music industry in ascendancy. China has built modern concert halls across the country and implemented an aggressive music-education program in schools. An estimated 20 million young Chinese have been hand-picked to study classical piano. U.S. conservatories such as Juilliard and Curtis are training the best of them.

Many of these young players are technically brilliant but critics are waiting for signs of deeper interpretations. Chinese-born Lang Lang, known by critics as Bang Bang, may be the first of many to grow into this role, and in the process to help pick up the slack in the Western classical tradition.

"In the less heady realm of small independent labels that are devoted exclusively or primarily to contemporary music, there are still plenty of new titles coming out every month, and still primarily on CDs."

Contemporary Classical Music Labels Are Healthy

Joseph Dalton

Joseph Dalton is an arts journalist and the author of Artists & Activists: Making Culture in New York's Capital Region. *In the following viewpoint he argues that small labels releasing contemporary classical music on CDs continue to thrive despite the drop in CD sales. Dalton notes that contemporary classical music has never had high sales. Labels exist to put out work they think is important, he says. Contemporary classical labels have always come and gone, but he concludes current labels continue to put out numerous discs of exciting music.*

As you read, consider the following questions:

1. Why does Dalton say that the economic bust is not being felt too strongly in upstate New York?

Joseph Dalton, "On Record—An Overview of the State of Contemporary Music Recording (Part 1): Still Spinning," NewMusicBox.org, July 8, 2009. Copyright © NewMusicBox 1998–2010. All rights reserved. Reproduced by permission.

2. According to the author, what did Other Mind Records grow out of?

3. Where is New Amsterdam records based, and how many discs had it released in the two years before Dalton's article?

"I am distressed about my CD sales, which have completely tanked. I talked to the head of my label about this, and he told me, 'No one's buying CDs.' In effect, he said, 'What makes you think you're special?' Everybody's collapsing."

—composer John Adams, Newsweek, February 5, 2009

"The recording industry is kaput."

—violinist Nadja Salerno-Sonnenberg, Times Union
(Albany, NY), February 8, 2007

You've heard the talk from lesser lights than these. It's said over and again: recordings are over and done with—except for all those CDs that keep getting released every month. It's similar to the even more familiar drone that nobody ever listens to contemporary music [that is, to contemporary classical, or concert, music]—except there's so much of it around all the time.

Small Labels, Many Titles

Certainly record stores are almost a thing of the past, with Tower Records and Virgin Megastores shuttered. Oh sure, there's still the music departments at Barnes & Noble and Borders, but just try to find much of a selection of contemporary music there. And the big multinational labels, which stars like Adams and Salerno-Sonnenberg once counted on, have indeed cut their artist rosters, slashed their recording budgets, and drastically curtailed their release schedules. Those operations, of course, are arms of corporations far more dependent upon mass sales of pop music to iPod-toting, file-sharing young people than on the always modest-sized audiences for symphonies, concertos, and string quartets, whether of new or old vintage.

But in the less heady realm of small independent labels that are devoted exclusively or primarily to contemporary music, there are still plenty of new titles coming out every month, and still primarily on CDs. In fact, a characteristic sense of perseverance and sometimes even some guarded optimism came through in recent interviews with a dozen managers of these plucky outfits.

The sense of the field garnered from researching this story brought to mind some recent casual conversations with small business owners in upstate New York, where I've lived for the past eight years. Because the economic boom never really came to this rather removed territory, the bust isn't being felt too strongly either. So it is with the recordings of new music.

"Business is booming and crackling," says Philip Blackburn, the composer who runs Innova Recordings, the 25-year-old recording arm of the American Composers Forum, based in Minnesota. "My desk is covered in submissions and my spare time in and out of the office is spent listening to them as well as catching up on infrastructure things."

Rather than looking to sales, Blackburn's barometer for business is typical of many who run independent labels: the demand from artists who want to make recordings. Innova is actually one of the surprisingly few labels with nonprofit status. But whatever their legal structure, most labels dedicated to contemporary music have as their first business focus the regular production of new titles; the subsequent sales of those discs is a secondary concern. Thus, a continual flow of new projects and the obtaining of funding to make them happen are essential. At Innova, 28 new titles were released last year and 23 are in the works for 2009. And the sales? Iffy, as always.

"It's a scramble to keep up with how things are changing," continues Blackburn. "Getting reviews and radio play that will get people to buy something, that's always been a long shot."

Finances at Contemporary Music Labels

It's a given: money has to come from somewhere before discs get released. It's just that the need for dough is more on the surface in all realms of the always-struggling little realm of contemporary American music. . . .

Scraping together the money to produce each new title and more often than not looking to the artists to help with that process—whether from family wealth, university research grants, or credit card debt—is standard operating procedure at almost every independent contemporary music label.

Joseph Dalton, NewMusicBox, July 13, 2009. www.newmusicbox.org.

Growing Interest

"Business is going very well," says Becky Starobin, who with her husband, the guitarist David Starobin, founded Bridge Records in 1981. "Orders are increasing, and our distribution network is expanding. We're getting more inquiries from different countries, which is quite remarkable in this climate. In addition to the major markets, we are now entering into agreements with smaller countries."

Starobin says that roughly 40 percent of Bridge titles are devoted to contemporary music, with the remainder consisting of baroque, classical, romantic, early 20th century, jazz, and world music. For 2009, there are 38 CDs slated for release. Just two years ago the annual release schedule was 30 titles.

"There has been a steady growth of interest," says Starobin. "I don't think we have experienced a boom since the late '80s and early '90s, but Bridge has certainly not experienced a bust. There are different avenues of distribution opening up, and it's our goal to make the music available to more and more people."

"We're holding our own," says Susan Bush of Albany Records, which was founded by Peter Kermani in 1987. Bush gets a palpable sense of the need to make recordings from artists, when eight to twelve submissions arrive just about every month. The label accepts about 60 percent of what comes in, she says. But that rate is nearly double what it was a few years ago because so many artists are returning to make second, third, and fourth projects with Albany. "We are working with people that we already know, who are sort of our stable of composers and performers," explains Bush.

Of course not every label operating today is sure and steady in its operations. Many are sole proprietorships dependent upon occasional grants and contributions as well as on the founder's continual infusions of time and interest.

Labels Come and Go

Keeping an eye on new music recordings has always included watching the labels come and go. For a trip down memory lane, check out *American Music Recordings: A Discography of 20th Century U.S. Composers*, a nearly 400-page tome edited by Carol Oja and released in 1982 by the Institute for Studies in American Music (recently renamed The H. Wiley Hitchcock Institute for Studies in American Music). Along with numerous citations of recordings on Victor, RCA, Columbia, and MGM—ah, the glory days when major labels cared!—there are also some long departed smaller operations like Desto, Turnabout, and Orion.

The last decade has also seen its share of failures in the field, including the venerable Composers Recordings Inc. [CRI], which had an honorable run from 1954 to 2003. (Full disclosure: I ran CRI from 1990 to 2000.) The catalog of CRI, including about 400 LPs and 300 CDs, is currently administered by New World Records. New World has thus far released eleven CD reissues of CRI titles, and the remainder of the CRI CD catalog is available through burn-on-demand CDs via the New World website.

Some labels born during the CD era have already come and gone. Composer Joseph Celli founded O.O. Discs in the mid-'90s and once maintained a rather active production schedule, but it was shuttered a number of years ago. And last year composer Richard Brooks brought to a close his Capstone Records, which he founded in 1985. In a brief recent email exchange, I asked Brooks whether his action was a retirement or just giving up. "A little of both," he replied. The Capstone imprint and its back catalog have been picked up by Parma Recordings, which also has two other labels, Navano for classics and Soundbrush for jazz and world.

In preparing the list of labels that accompanies this article, email inquiries were sent to about 60 labels in order to ascertain their level of current activity. At least half the companies never responded. Overly stringent email filters and the busy and distracted lives of composer/performer/entrepreneurs are understandable, so if the label had a relatively current website, we included them on the list. Still, some companies seem to be missing in action or dormant. The Santa Fe Music Group, which was primarily devoted to reissuing on CD the analog era recordings of the Louisville Orchestra, couldn't be found. Opus One has a shell of a web site. And the "new" releases on Newport Classic's site appear to be two to three years old, based on cross references to Amazon. So it goes.

The steadfastness, both emotional and financial, necessary to keep a label going may be hard won, but the artistic vision and ambition to start one are easily had. Likewise, the learning curve to produce presentable discs and booklets is not steep. Thus, the menu of labels continues to expand.

There have always been record collectors who, late in life, spend some of their savings to finally take their crack at being "record men." And plenty of composers have set up shop over the years, including Gunther Schuller with GM Recordings in 1981, Max Lifchitz with North/South in 1992, and John Zorn with Tzadik in 1995.

Other Minds and BMOP

Many of the latest entries into the field emerged from an existing music organization or emerging artistic scene. In San Francisco, Other Minds Records was launched in 1998 as an outgrowth of the then six-year-old Other Minds Festival. Composer Charles Amirkhanian uses an oft-repeated term when describing the value of recordings: "The CDs doubled as calling cards," he says, adding that they were first used as premium gifts for donors. Beyond its use as a promotional vehicle for the festival, Amikhanian's rationale for the label is also a familiar refrain among those who decide to start their own shop: "We realized that a number of really interesting kinds of music were falling between the cracks and that no one else was going to release them." While the Other Minds Festival presents living composers, often performing their own works, Other Minds Records, now with 17 titles, has hewed toward rare and out of print repertoire, such as recordings of the late George Antheil performing his own music, the player piano rolls of Conlon Nancarrow (reissued from 1750 Arch), and the most recent release featuring early works of Marc Blitzstein.

Last year conductor Gil Rose and his 12-year-old Boston Modern Orchestra Project [BMOP] decided it was time to strike out on their own after making some 20 recordings for other labels. "We were conceiving the CDs and raising the money, doing the rehearsing and performing, as well as the recording and post production, and then handing off the masters for nothing or very little compared to what the costs were in cash and blood, sweat, and tears," says Rose. "The final straw came when we started doing the cover designs, which we asked to do because we were getting some unattractive covers."

BMOP/sound already has 12 titles, each attractively presented in cardboard packaging, and each presenting the work of a single composer. They include music of Charles Fussell, Derek Bermel, Lee Hyla, and David Rakowski. And the label is committed to an on-going release schedule of one new disc per month. While Rose likes the comparison to the Louisville Orchestra's trenchant recording work during the LP era, he concedes that not every project features big orchestral pieces, though the growing catalog already includes operas by John Harbison and Eric Sawyer. "[The label] mirrors the BMOP mission. I stuck this word 'project' in the name and I still get flack for it, but I wanted to convey that we're fluid and flexible. At BMOP performances, sometimes there are 90 people on stage and sometimes 15, and sometimes that's in the same concert. It's a very chameleon-like ensemble," explains Rose. "You can send CDs all over the world, but you can't get everyone into Jordan Hall. The label has expanded our network and visibility in almost every way."

New Amsterdam Records

From the latest generation of composer/performers in New York comes New Amsterdam Records, founded by William Brittelle, Judd Greenstein, and Sarah Kirkland Snider, all composers in their early 30s with advanced degrees in music. They've been busy, releasing 16 discs in less than two years. Some of the latest titles include Darcy James Argue's *Infernal Machines*, featuring his 18-piece "steampunk big band" Secret Society, and Brittelle's own *Mohair Time Warp*, with the composer singing above a hyperactive mix of amplified chamber ensemble and wailing electric guitars.

"The idea to start a cool record label mainly grew out of this developing genre of music that was coming from people with great educations in composition but who were also influenced by pop music and jazz and didn't fit into any strict marketplace," explains Greenstein. "The music industry is a place where you're either popular or classical. Everything forces you to one side or the other. We want to stay in the middle."

Greenstein recalls telling composer Michael Gordon, cofounder of Bang on a Can, which has its own label, Cantaloupe Music, of the plan to start New Amsterdam. "He tried to convince me it was a terrible idea, that it would take a lot of time from composing," says Greenstein. "He was coming from a positive place and he was right. Our careers have suffered because of much less time to write music. But the (industry) system we're operating in is broken from our perspective. It doesn't meet our needs."

"I thought there was more risk not [to start the label]," says Brittelle. "When I got out of school, I wanted to spend all day writing music and anything else was a distraction. But coming into the office every day, even on my flexible schedule, has been great for me as a composer. It keeps me in touch and bombarded by great ideas. And there's a healthy sense of competition because you'll hear a great record by a friend and it helps you stay in reality, and to know what it takes to really get something out there in the market place. You've got to pack up a van [for a gig] but also pack up recordings and mail them."

Periodical and Internet Sources Bibliography

The following articles have been selected to supplement the diverse views presented in this chapter.

Jace Clayton	"Pitch Perfect," *Frieze*, May 2009.
Economist	"Classical Music: Reports of Its Death Are Exaggerated," March 3, 2007.
Adam R. Gold	"Death of Auto-Tune," *Harvard Crimson*, March 11, 2011.
Tom Huizenga	"Symphonic Resolutions: What's Broken in Classical Music, and How Do We Fix It?," *Deceptive Cadence* blog, January 17, 2011. www.npr.org.
Helienne Lindvall	"Behind the Music: Why We Need HMV," *Guardian* (Manchester, UK), January 7, 2011.
Mike Masnick	"Songwriters Guild Claims the Internet Makes It Impossible to Create Content," TechDirt, May 4, 2010. www.techdirt.com.
Andrew Matson	"Inventor of Auto-Tune: 'I'm Innocent!,'" *Matson on Music* blog, June 26, 2009. http://seattletimes .nwsource.com.
Anne Midgette	"CD Industry [or] Bust?," *Classical Beat* blog, August 17, 2009. http:// voices.washingtonpost.com.
Jonathan Miller	"Struggling to Shake Off Its Past," *New York Times*, April 9, 2006.
Anna Pulley	"Is Auto-Tune Killing Pop Music?," *Mother Jones*, May 17, 2010.
Josh Tyrangiel	"Auto-Tune: Why Pop Music Sounds Perfect," *Time*, February 5, 2009.

For Further Discussion

Chapter 1

1. Copyright law used to protect works for thirty-four years from the time of the creation of the work. Today, copyright generally extends for the life of the author plus another seventy years. Based on your reading of the viewpoints in this chapter, what do you think a fair length of copyright would be? What concerns would you try to balance in establishing length of copyright?

2. Based on the readings, do you think that sampling a song without permission or using portions of someone else's song without permission is the same as stealing? Is it wrong but not as bad as stealing? Is it perfectly acceptable? Explain your reasoning.

Chapter 2

1. Would you or your friends buy more (or any) CDs if the price were lower? What do you think is a fair price for a CD? Why?

2. Imagine you are starting out as a musician. On the basis of the viewpoints in this chapter, what are some of the ways in which you might try to make a living? What are some of the problems with each of the methods you come up with?

Chapter 3

1. Brent Defore argues that only major labels can get artists a big house, a fancy car, and all the perks of stardom. Is this a good justification for all or most artists to sign with major labels? Why or why not?

2. Based on the viewpoints in this chapter, what advantages are there to releasing music independently on your own,

without a label? What advantages might there be to releasing music through a label?

Chapter 4

1. What is your favorite music album? Would the album be somehow less good if you were able to download only portions of it? If the main format for music shifts from albums to singles, would that be a loss or a gain for music? Explain your answers in light of the viewpoint by Steven Hodson.

2. Do you agree that the decline in orchestra patronage and funding described by Johnson is attributable to anti-intellectualism: What do you make of Joseph Dalton's contrasting claims about the health of the classical music recording industry?

Organizations to Contact

The editors have compiled the following list of organizations concerned with the issues debated in this book. The descriptions are derived from materials provided by the organizations. All have publications or information available for interested readers. The list was compiled on the date of publication of the present volume; names, addresses, phone and fax numbers, and e-mail and Internet addresses may change. Be aware that many organizations take several weeks or longer to respond to inquiries, so allow as much time as possible.

American Federation of Musicians of the United States and Canada (AFM)

1501 Broadway, Suite 600
New York, NY 10036
(212) 869-1330 • fax: (212) 764-6134
e-mail: presoffice@afm.org
website: www.afm.org

The American Federation of Musicians of the United States and Canada is the largest organization in the world representing the interests of professional musicians. The organization negotiates fair agreements, protects ownership of recorded music, secures benefits such as health care and pensions, and lobbies legislators. AFM publishes the magazine *International Musician*.

American Society of Composers, Authors and Publishers (ASCAP)

1 Lincoln Plaza
New York, NY 10023
(212) 621-6000; toll-free: (800) 95-ASCAP • fax: (212) 621-8453
e-mail: info@ascap.com
website: www.ascap.com

The American Society of Composers, Authors and Publishers is a membership association of more than 330,000 US composers, songwriters, lyricists, and music publishers. ASCAP protects the rights of its members by licensing and distributing royalties for the nondramatic public performances of their copyrighted works. ASCAP publishes the *ASCAP Advantage*.

Electronic Frontier Foundation (EFF)
454 Shotwell Street
San Francisco, CA 94110-1914
(415) 436-9333 • fax: (415) 436-9993
e-mail: information@eff.org
website: www.eff.org.

The Electronic Frontier Foundation is a small, grassroots legal advocacy nonprofit supported by member contributions. The organization specializes in cases in which it can help shape law in the areas of digital freedom, including more consumer-friendly file-sharing rules. Its website offers a blog with the latest news of "the electronic frontier," as well as press releases and other information.

Future of Music Coalition (FMC)
1615 L Street NW, #520
Washington, DC 20036
(202) 822-2051
e-mail: summit@futureofmusic.org
website: www.futureofmusic.org

The Future of Music Coalition is a not-for-profit collaboration between members of the music, technology, public policy, and intellectual property law communities that seeks to bring together diverse voices to identify and find creative solutions to the new challenges of technology. The FMC generates research on the music industry and publishes articles as well as the *FMC Newsletter*.

International Federation of the Phonographic Industry (IFPI)

10 Piccadilly Circus
London W1J 0DD UK
+44 (0)20 7878 7900 • fax: +44 (0)20 7878 7950
e-mail: info@ifpi.org
website: www.ifpi.org

The International Federation of the Phonographic Industry is an organization representing the recording industry worldwide. Its mission is to promote the value of recorded music, safeguard the rights of record producers, and expand the commercial uses of recorded music. It works to enforce antipiracy legislation, to lobby governments, and to provide authoritative market research and information. It publishes numerous reports about the music industry, including the annual *IFPI Digital Music Report* and the annual *Recording Industry in Numbers*.

Just Plain Folks Songwriting/Musician Networking Organization

5327 Kit Drive
Indianapolis, IN 46237
e-mail: justplainfolks@aol.com
website: www.jpfolks.com

Just Plain Folks is a networking group for people in the music industry, including musicians, journalists, and retailers. The organization facilitates online networking as well as face-to-face meetings. Its website offers a member database, blog, and news about the music industry.

National Music Publishers' Association (NMPA)

975 F Street NW, Suite 375
Washington, DC 20004
(202) 393-6672
e-mail: pr@nmpa.org
website: www.nmpa.org

The National Music Publishers' Association is the largest US music publishing trade association. NMPA represents its members to protect their property rights on the legislative, litigation, and regulatory fronts. NMPA publishes the newsletter *NMPA News and Views*.

The Recording Academy
3030 Olympic Blvd.
Santa Monica, CA 90404
(310) 392-3777 • fax: (310) 399-3090
e-mail: memservices@grammy.com
website: www.grammy.com

The Recording Academy's mission is "to positively impact the lives of musicians, industry members and our society at large." The group's work focuses on advocacy, music education, and philanthropy. The Recording Academy is also known for presenting the Grammy Awards. The group publishes *Grammy Magazine*.

Recording Industry Association of America (RIAA)
1025 F Street NW, 10th Floor
Washington, DC 20004
(202) 775-0101
website: www.riaa.com

The Recording Industry Association of America is the trade group that represents the US recording industry. The organization protects the intellectual property rights of artists and is the official certification agency for gold, platinum, and multiplatinum sales awards. RIAA publishes the newsletter *Fast Tracks*.

Songwriters Guild of America (SGA)
5120 Virginia Way, Suite C22
Nashville, TN 37207
(615) 742-9945; toll-free: (800) 524-6742 • fax: (615) 630-7501
e-mail: nash@songwritersguild.com

website: www.songwritersguild.com

Songwriters Guild of America is a songwriters' association that advocates on issues of importance to songwriters and the music industry in general, including home taping, derivative rights, authors' moral rights, and, most recently, infringement of royalty payments due to digital/Internet piracy. The group works on lobbying, talking with the media, and negotiating and coordinating with other industry groups. SGA publishes the newsletter *Songwriters Guild of America*.

Bibliography of Books

Alan Bargfrede

Music Law in the Digital Age. Boston: Berklee, 2009.

Randy Chertkow
and Jason Feehan

The Indie Band Survival Guide: The Manual for the Do-It-Yourself Musician. New York: St. Martin's, 2008.

Joanna Demers

Steal This Music: How Intellectual Property Law Affects Musical Creativity. Athens: University of Georgia Press, 2006.

Nathan W. Fisk

Understanding Online Piracy: The Truth About Illegal File Sharing. Santa Barbara, CA: ABC-CLIO, 2009.

Fred Goodman

Fortune's Fool: Edgar Bronfman, Jr., Warner Music, and an Industry in Crisis. New York: Simon & Schuster, 2010.

Sameer Hinduja

Music Piracy and Crime Theory. El Paso, TX: LFB, 2006.

Mark Katz

Capturing Sound: How Technology Has Changed Music. Rev. ed. Berkeley and Los Angeles: University of California Press, 2010.

Mike King

Music Marketing: Press, Promotion, Distribution, and Retail. Boston: Berklee, 2009.

Steve Knopper	*Appetite for Self-Destruction: The Spectacular Crash of the Record Industry in the Digital Age.* New York: Simon & Schuster, 2009.
Greg Kot	*Ripped: How the Wired Generation Revolutionized Music.* New York: Scribner, 2009.
Lawrence Kramer	*Why Classical Music Still Matters.* Berkeley and Los Angeles: University of California Press, 2007.
David Kusek and Gerd Leonhard	*The Future of Music: Manifesto for the Digital Revolution.* Boston: Berklee, 2005.
Norman Lebrecht	*Who Killed Classical Music? Maestros, Managers, and Corporate Politics.* New York: Birch Lane, 1997.
Greil Marcus and Daphne Carr, eds.	*Best Music Writing 2009.* Cambridge, MA: Da Capo, 2009.
Kembrew McLeod and Peter DiCola	*Creative License: The Law and Culture of Digital Sampling.* Durham, NC: Duke University Press, 2011.
Andre Millard	*America on Record: A History of Recorded Sound.* 2nd ed. New York: Cambridge University Press, 2005.
Paul D. Miller	*Sound Unbound: Sampling Digital Music and Culture.* Cambridge, MA: MIT Press, 2008.
David J. Moser	*Moser on Music Copyright.* Vallejo, CA: Artistpro, 2006.

Bobby Owsinski	*The Touring Musician's Handbook.* Milwaukee: Hal Leonard, 2011.
Ann Powers and Daphne Carr, eds.	*Best Music Writing 2010.* Cambridge, MA: Da Capo, 2010.
Daylle Deanna Schwartz	*Start and Run Your Own Record Label.* 3rd ed. New York: Billboard Books, 2009.
Aram Sinnreich	*Mashed Up: Music, Technology, and the Rise of Configurable Culture.* Amherst: University of Massachusetts Press, 2010.
Brian Southall	*The Rise & Fall of EMI Records.* London: Omnibus, 2009.
Frances Vincent	*Myspace for Musicians: The Comprehensive Guide to Marketing Your Music.* Boston: Course Technology, 2010.
Patrik Wikstrom	*The Music Industry: Music in the Cloud.* Malden, MA: Polity, 2009.

Index